The withered oak stands upright in the storm,
The healthy tree is shattered to the ground
Because the wind can grasp it by the crown.

Heinrich von Kleist

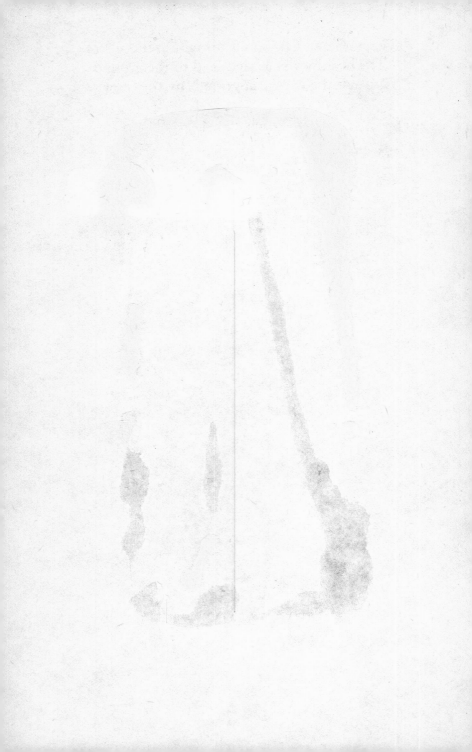

Heinrich von Kleist
1777/1977

by

Curt Hohoff

1977   Inter Nationes
Bonn-Bad Godesberg

Documentary and bibliographical appendix edited by Paul Raabe
Bibliography newly revised by Elisabeth Raabe

Translated by Patricia Crampton, London

Originally published under the title of Kleist in the series
"rowohlts monographien"
© Rowohlt Taschenbuch Verlag GmbH, Reinbek near Hamburg, 1958
In collaboration with Inter Nationes, Bonn-Bad Godesberg
Layout: Heinz Bähr, Cologne
Overall production: Bonner Universitäts-Buchdruckerei, Bonn
Printed in the Federal Republic of Germany 1977

Contents

The Kleist Phenomenon

Heinrich von Kleist is the writer of the turn — the turn from the outlook of German Classicism to the present day. He is neither an emotionalist nor an idealist. The world and life no longer have any definite and definable meaning for him, they are "brittle", a riddle, a delusion. What is called reality is neither governed nor permeated by an idea; it is the uncanny partner of the individual human being. Its laws are confusing, crazed and sinister, indeed unfathomable, and the clearer this becomes, the lonelier the individual feels. There is a God, there are gods, but they belong to this world and take part in the confusion of men. So man must cling to the ego, to his awareness of himself. Alkmene withstands the confrontation with the god until he bows in admiration before his creation. Penthesilea sees the world as a tormented road to death in which she will at last mature. The Prince of Homburg sees his own grave and is shaken by an existential shudder, unknown to Classicism, which makes him "free".

Kleist himself was a riddle. A character and an artist on the grand scale, slowly destroyed by scruples and doubts. A dual structure of chastity and licence, hardness and yieldingness, fairytale reverie and violent resolve, has led to his character being described as pathological. This is true insofar as modern man is in general anomalous, being and awareness, falling asunder.

For reasons of family tradition Kleist began as a soldier, turning subsequently to literature. National feeling never constrained him; only the despotism of a military government which was becoming insupportable awakened the patriot. Then indeed he found words against the enemy, of such daemonic greatness that at thirty Kleist was able to appear as the ideal opponent to stand against a Napoleon. The nineteenth century held fast to this image: Kleist appeared as "the" Prussian writer, which is paradoxical, since the king regarded Kleist as a traitor and rebel; the *Prince of Homburg* was not allowed to be performed in Prussia because a general falls senseless in it.

Kleist was ambitious, he always wanted the highest, he wanted to wrest the laurels from Goethe's head in order to be the greatest poet. In many respects he completed Schiller's work and transcended Goethe's intentions. Goethe turned against him because he sensed that this young man drew conclusions from which he had turned his face in horror since Weimar. The spirit of self-destructions was always alive in Kleist, leading him into thoughts of suicide, which in the end he carried out. The opposite pole in him was his need for peace. For years he hoped to be able to become a farmer. He liked the old Zoroastrian saying: To plant a tree, to kill an enemy, to conceive a child were most worthy of a man. Where is the unity of these demands? It lies beyond Kleist, it is that charm he sought and now and then possessed in life. His mad pretension was balanced by a child-like simplicity, even humility.

Certain themes constantly recur in Kleist, in which symbols of his ambivalent outlook may be seen. In Würzburg, for instance, he was gripped by the sight of a domed tower, held static by the fact that every stone would in itself be inclined to fall. Another theme is that of the mighty oak which falls because the storm can grasp its crown, whereas the rotten tree stands; this theme occurs in the letters, in the *Familie Schroffenstein* and at the end of *Penthesilea*. Paradoxical images, which would have been as senseless in the sphere of Schiller's drama as in Goethe. Yet Kleist did not become a cynic and

The house in Frankfurt an der Oder where Kleist was born

nihilist like so many Romantics, for he retained a deep belief that truth and purity must exist somewhere. This was responsible for the indescribable nobility of his work. His witnesses are verse and style, harmony of language and greatness of dramatic scope beyond all possible expectation.

All Kleist's heroes, the corpus of his work, transcend Kleist's own restlessly restricted life. Just as his own personality was always a riddle to him, so his life cannot explain his work. That is why Kleistian scholarship has not flourished very widely. In the 1920's a number of books appeared which broadly grasped and presented the phenomenon, and it was only then that people began to see that Kleist was neither Classicist nor Romantic, no nationalist Prussian patriot but one of the first

Heinrich von Kleist aged 7, with his mother
(coloured miniature on ivory, by Franz Ludwig Klose)

modern men of Germany. Grace and despair are interlaced with one another, the earthly and the divine are insidiously separated and locked up. There is evidence of this in such touching characters as Toni and Käthchen, and in his violent way Kohlhaas speaks of the same thing. In this brittle world there are constantly points where paradise becomes visible: in love, whose place is the leaves, the cave, the bed and finally — more mysterious and pregnant than them all — death.

But Kleist's devotion to being was also his faith and this distinguishes it from the naked pessimism and nihilism of the century following him. However, he could find no words for it other than in the people of his plays, in Alkmene, Penthesilea and Käthchen. Besides Goethe, he is the poet of profound and true women; they are the personification of a generally slumbering image of truth and purity. He had departed at an early stage from orthodox belief; in Würzburg and Dresden he had intimations of a Christian whole, in his greatest dramas he touches so closely here and there on the mysteries of Christianity that there has been no lack of attempts to call the truth of his work a Christian truth. Undoubtedly Kleist was seeking a synthesis transcending all concepts; he represents himself literarily in *Amphitryon* and the *Prince of Homburg*.

Youth

There are two poets called Kleist in German literature, both members of the same family. Ewald Christian von Kleist, 1715—1759, was a reluctant officer and he too had a fiancée called Wilhelmine, whom he did not marry. He too was a poet. He died as the result of a wound suffered in the Battle of Kunersdorf. As a writer he was a friend of Gleim and Lessing. Measured against that of Heinrich von Kleist, his poetry seems sweet, almost soft, with an antique tendency. He gave of his best in wonderfully resounding, often unrhymed idylls. Nature consoled him, so too did the thought of friendship. Lessing erected his memorial when he gave Major Tellheim in "Minna von Barnhelm" the features of the fallen Major von Kleist.

The Kleist family came from Pomerania and was originally, no doubt, of Slavic origin. It became one of the great officer families of the Prussian state and even by Heinrich von Kleist's time it had produced twenty generals and field-marshals. A Lieutenant-General Franz Kasimir von Kleist was at that time Infantry Inspector in the March, and ceded Magdeburg to the French without a struggle; the family honour seemed to have been violated and his nephew suffered for it in Austria. A Georg Friedrich Otto von Kleist was Director of the École Militaire in Berlin. The poet's father was Joachim Friedrich von Kleist and succeeded in rising to Company Commander in Frankfurt-on-the-Oder. He died at the age of 60, when his son Bernd Wilhelm Heinrich was eleven years old. Kleist was born on 18 October 1777.

Captain von Kleist's first wife was Karoline Luise von Wulfen, who bore him two daughters, Wilhelmine and Ulrike, Kleist's favourite half-sister. His second wife was Juliane Ulrike von Pannwitz. The children of this marriage were called Friederike, Auguste, Heinrich, Leopold and Juliane. Leopold von Kleist, the poet's only brother, retired as a senior officer and became postmaster in Stolp in Pomerania; his descendants are still living now. The family was not landed but its revenues allowed it to live in keeping with its rank. It was fully within the army tradition of Frederick the Great. Kleist's mother was eighteen years younger than his father but she died in 1793, five years after her husband. An aunt took charge of the household.

Later Kleist did not speak kindly of his upbringing in the parental home. It seems to have been rigid, formal, orthodox Lutheran and impersonal. After his father's death Heinrich was passed on to Parson Katel as a boarder in Berlin. At 15, in accordance with family tradition, he entered the Potsdam Regiment of Guards. He served with the regiment from 1792—1799,

Portrait of the young Heinrich von Kleist
(Painter unknown. Berlin, in private ownership)

as a Lieutenant from 1797 onwards. When his mother died he was given leave for the funeral; at that time the earliest surviving letter from Kleist was written to his aunt on his return to his Regiment in March 1793. The Regiment was stationed in Frankfurt-am-Main, engaged on the Rhine campaign in the war against the French Revolution. Kleist was 16. The adventures in the post-carriage are vividly described. Kleist was a young gentleman, member of a famous regiment and therefore a man of the world, but at the same time still a boy, climbing the ruins of a fortress by the roadside. The episode of a bandit who had jumped onto the back of the carriage and was scared off by a whip is a dramatic postscript. Kleist saw a great deal, knew much of the history, experienced the landscape with astonishing intensity and knew how to describe it, but grammatically his German was uncertain.

The campaign ended after the Siege of Mainz with the Peace of Basel. The Regiment returned to the Potsdam garrison, where they wore stiff collars and compulsory uniforms and as future officers would have a servant, but led a life deep in the strictest conventions of the Service and of private life. The common language was French, especially in the company of ladies. How happy Kleist must have been when he could escape the drillground; an opportunity arose through a trip taken with friends to the Harz, strictly incognito, disguised as musicians; it was claimed afterwards that they earned their bread by playing. With friends such as Rühle von Lilienstern and Pfuel, Kleist had a musical "coronet" and played the clarinet. He was highly musical, as shown by his famous statements on musical theory. A little later came the *Essay to Find the Certain Way of Happiness and Enjoy it Undisturbed Even Among the Greatest Tribulations of Life.* Here the happy events of the Harz journey are given a moral application. Its expression is dedicated to the jargon of the Enlightenment. One can already feel that Kleist has discovered his want of the naive desire for life. It will be difficult for the respected middle way to be the author's way — otherwise he would not have recommended it so insistently.

Heinrich and his step-sister Ulrike von Kleist (miniatures)

Officer of the Guards Regiment, 2nd and 3rd Batallions, to which Kleist
belonged

Kleist was at that time working particularly on mathematics and geometry. The popular scientific writers of the Enlightenment were addicted to the "pure" sciences; Kleist gave thought to problems of pure mathematics and here he seems to have been tormented as to whether one human being should trust another's conviction more than his own; *I say a thinking human being!* A man with such a question must find the soldier's state problematical, depending as it does on command and blind obedience. The roots of Kleist's criticism of the profession he adopted according to family tradition lie in himself. All the reasons he adduces against the soldier's life are those of a heart in need of its own truth and self-realization. There is no question of literature, though he may read Wieland's *Sympathien*; it was appropriate to his age and sensitivity.

In Potsdam Kleist spent most of his time in two houses, that of his cousin Marie von Kleist and that of Frau Adolphine von Werdeck. Marie von Kleist, née von Gualtieri, was sixteen years older than her cousin. She had been married since 1792 to Major Friedrich Wilhelm Christian von Kleist, from whom she was guiltlessly divorced after twenty years of marriage. She belonged to Queen Luise's intimate circle and was one of the few people who later helped Kleist. She appealed to the king on his behalf several times and obtained a small pension for him when he was without means. After Kleist's death she wrote: "In Heinrich Kleist I have lost the partner in all my joys and in all my sorrows." Marie von Kleist was cultured well beyond the average. Kleist wrote her the last and loveliest letters of his life.

The Werdecks were part of the court nobility. Adolphine (1772—1844) a merry lady, feared in Potsdam for her sharp tongue, lived in chilly wedlock with her husband, who was divorced in 1812. She seems to have known Kleist even before the Rhineland campaign, since letters were exchanged. It is highly probable that she was the object of a boyish adoration and kept her passionate friend, who was five years younger, away from the loose girls of that soldiers' town. Kleist constantly resumed, indeed sought a renewed relationship with her

16

over many years. In 1803 she made quite a long journey via Weimar through Switzerland and northern Italy to Paris, during which Kleist met her several times.

The more Kleist grew away from his officer's career, the more he began to see as his ideal *educating* (himself) *into a scholar,* and teaching or working in a scholarly capacity. It was these ideas which made him write his great confessional letter of 18/19 March 1799 to his former teacher Ernst Martini. Everything on which he asks his friend and former teacher for advice was already decided; this was Kleist's monologue with himself. We must also see Kleist's lost *Ideenmagazin,* his lost diary and his similarly lost *Roman meiner Seele* as in the same category as this letter[1]. We read:

"But in order to put you in a position to reach a proper verdict, I shall have to range rather more widely and therefore reiterate my plea for patience, since I foresee that the subject and the extent of its contemplation will carry me away.

Without searching for the more distant causes of my decision, we can linger straight away over those from which it immediately flows: the wish for happiness.

This is a natural reason and at the same time to a certain extent the only one, because in the right sense it comprises all my other reasons within itself.

The whole of our investigation will be restricted to the investigation of this wish alone and in order to place you in a position to judge it, it will be necessary to establish the concept of happiness and true benefit. But here I meet at once with a great difficulty; for the concepts of happiness are as different as

---

[1] Kleist not only used certain symbols and images time and again in almost exactly the same words, but in his letters to different people identical descriptions occur. In letters and stories there are parallel passages and terms which cannot be explained only by a good memory but must have been copied down in each case. The substrate of these copies was the *Ideenmagazin* which may be identical with the diary.

the tastes and senses with which they are enjoyed. To one it is excess, and where, my friend, can this wish be fulfilled, where can happiness be better founded than in that place where the instruments of enjoyment, our senses, lie, to which all creation refers, in which the world with its infinite charms is repeated in little. There too it is our property alone, it does not depend on external circumstances, no tyrant can rob us of it, no villain destroy it; we carry it with us the world over.

These considerations, which I repeat to myself frequently and with pleasure, delight me in every one of my imaginings of them, because I feel with all my soul how true they are and how powerfully they favour and support my decision. So I incessantly practise the separation of true happiness from all external circumstances and attach it only as reward and encouragement to virtue. There it appears in more beautiful form and on surer ground.

Of course, when I visualize happiness as the reward of virtue, I think of the first as the end and the second only as the means. At the same time I feel that in this sense virtue does not appear in its highest dignity, although I cannot suggest how the faulty relationship in this idea might be altered. It is possible that it is the property of a few rather beautiful souls: to love virtue for virtue's sake alone . . ."

A little later, in the same letter, we read:

"Happiness I actually call only the full and extravagant delights which — to give it to you at a stroke — lie in the pleasurable contemplation of the moral beauty of our own being. These delights, the satisfaction with ourself, the consciousness of good actions, the feeling of our own worth which we have steadfastly maintained in every moment of our lives, perhaps against a thousand challenges and temptations, are capable, in all the external circumstances of life, even under those apparently most tragic, of establishing a sure, deeply felt, indestructible happiness. And surely, with these concepts of

18

happiness, wealth, goods, worth and all the fragile gifts of chance, they equally deserve the name?"

The tone and style of these declarations betray Kleist's innocence; they correspond to the convention of that time when one could converse of happiness and virtue as we can of technical matters today. It is the pattern of a by-gone world. The humanism of German Classicism appeared then to Schlegel, Tieck and Novalis as a historical phase, overtaken by their own literary revolution. Kleist still regarded *moral education* as the *most sacred duty* and soon we read in letters to his sister of his *life's plan*: "To live without a plan of life is to expect chance to make us happy as we ourselves cannot do."

His family thought this was all theory. They were not interested in the new life's plan of the seeker of moral happiness and suggested that if he were going to become a student, it should be of something useful, jurisprudence or economics (then known as Kameralia, the subject in vogue at the turn of the century. Brentano, Adam Müller, Arnim, Novalis and the Eichendorff brothers, as well as the Grimm brothers, were studying Kameralia and Jus — not the science of literature). Kleist agreed. It was his only opportunity of getting out of his uniform jacket. He did not want people to realise what was going on in his soul, of what "beautiful impressions" it was capable. Once again, it is not literature he means here, but the moral perfecting of the ego, the possessions of "truth", which appeared to him as an abstract, self-respect. He put it confidentially to Ulrike, the only relation allowed to hear of such a thing, that both of them had lost the Christian religion of childhood and must try to gain a new one: it could be none other than that of the happiness of virtue.

At the same time Kleist discovered that he was speaking with difficulty and could not express himself with the skill and speed he would have liked. He felt insecure in society because he had not that ready tongue which one must have to be of any account there; he could not bear taking part in the conventional loquacity on every subject in chatty conversations. His later essay *On the Gradual Preparation of Thoughts while Speaking* (1805) presents a problem he had himself suffered; but one should not conclude that Kleist stuttered or that any speech defect motivated his Würzburg journey. Social conversation is neither objectively true, nor does what one says there come from the heart; therefore it was bound to leave a man in search of self-respect and moral seriousness unsatisfied. His goal was not education for conventional society. Kleist wrote to Ulrike:

"I often tell myself for my comfort that my goal is not education for society, that this education and my goal are two quite different paths towards quite different states of cultivation — for if, for instance, one goal is reached by much social intercourse, much chatter, by assurance and superficiality, the other is attained only through loneliness, thought, caution and thoroughness. Even though my conduct now should not please, the goal I have in mind should be considered foolish, I should be laughed at in the streets I wander, as Columbus was laughed at because he looked West for the East Indies . . ."

In the autumn of 1799, after taking leave, Kleist was studying in Frankfurt-an-der-Oder. Through his sisters he met the daughter of the local Commandant, Wilhelmine von Zenge, a conventionally educated, pretty girl and he was soon on fire; they got engaged. A demon had come to an angel. Wilhelmine became the recipient of the strangest engagement letters known to literature, wonderful letters, in which a young man, whose name is also Heinrich von Kleist, talks to himself about his fiancée. There is no talk of love here, no trace of sensuality, indeed there is a grotesque exaggeration of doubt as to this love.

How is a feeling, love, to be certain of the love of another being? Is there really any way from Me to You? Is not every man locked up in himself as in a prison? Here the conflicts of the poet of troubled love germinate:

J. J. Otto August Rühle von Lilienstern, a friend of Kleist's youth

Wilhelmine von Zenge, Kleist's fiancée (silhouette)

(the beginning is missing) ". . . visibly the certainty of being loved by you? Does not the happy self-awareness of requited and fortunate love breathe in every line? And yet — who has told me of it? And where has it been written?

Of course — what else should I conclude from the joyousness which has filled you too since yesterday, from the tears of joy you shed at your father's declaration, from the sweetness with which you have sometimes looked at me in these past days, what should I conclude from the intimate confidence with which you spoke to me in some of these past evenings, especially yesterday at the pianoforte, what from the boldness, with which you now, because you may, approach me even in the presence of others, where you had always shyly stood apart from me before — I ask, what should I conclude from all these almost unmistakable expressions, what else, Wilhelmine, than that I am loved?

But may I really trust my eyes and my ears? May I trust my wits and my perception, may I trust the feelings of my credulous heart, which has already been deceived by similar expressions? Should I not be mistrustful of my conclusions, since you yourself have already shown me how false they sometimes are?"

Kleist set his fiancée exercises on the following pattern: "If both man and wife do for each other what they can according to their nature, which of the two loses most when one dies first?" He put the question: "Which is more desirable, to have been happy for a short time or not at all?" And gives the answer himself. He wants to educate his fiancée on his lines, basically he does not see a You at all, to whom one lovingly confides oneself, but holds his inner monologue with a being which cannot defend itself.

The *Essay On The Certain Way of Finding Happiness,* originally written for Rühle in Potsdam, was now finished. Parts of it contain literal echoes of Wieland's *Sympathien* and quotations from Schiller's *Don Carlos:* "Suffering injustice flatters great souls." Lieutenant von Kleist had scarcely known of Schiller, now he experienced powerful influences from him. In Berlin he bought *Wallenstein* as soon as it appeared. The friend, Brockes, with whom he planned to undertake a secret journey was to be his Marquis Posa.

The Würzburg Journey
(Rousseau, Kant)

As a thinker, Kleist the bridegroom moved along the path of Wolff, Mendelssohn, Abbt, Iselin and Lessing. The establishment of a Plan of Life and the doctrine that for the thinking individual, happiness would inevitably yield itself, are their postulates. Kleist gave lectures from a pulpit to the ladies of his acquaintance on this and similar topics: To the ascetic state of happiness, virtue rather than enjoyment is the most important thing. Kleist knew exactly what the world was like and how people behaved in it. He knew how to define the obligations of married people towards each other and did not hesitate to restrict the husband's duties by the demands made by the state on the man, so "that ultimately the man is not always happy when the wife is, the wife, conversely, is always happy if the man is happy". His Eros was directed towards knowledge rather than his bride. A lover could not behave more passionately in wooing a maiden than Kleist wooed the sciences. With overwhelming haste the retired Lieutenant, homeless thanks to his departure from the social structure of the Army, tried to build himself a new world, for he by no means slid into literature or bohemianism. Although he had already broken with proud traditions, he intended to exchange them for a higher world, that of the mind.

The connection between the spiritual nature of man and his animal nature — a topic which the young Schiller discussed with academic thoroughness — could not be satisfactorily resolved for a young engaged man, since it is this very natural restriction and limitation which is Eros's way. Ascetic demands were opposed to the hedonistic tendencies of the age, whose poet Wieland was. Kleist knew precisely what he had to do: logic prescribed a formula for his thinking and if pursued correctly, the answers arose by themselves; the idea that one might be thinking badly, misguidedly, even wrongly, was, as it were, an unfair assumption. The opposition was not exhausted in the conceptual pair "enjoyment-duty". Like his relation Ewald von Kleist, the poet of the Frederican Age, suffering from the dichotomy between officer and man but remaining a soldier, since a poor nobleman had no opportunities in civil life, Kleist suffered from his self-elected homelessness. This explains the fervour with which he flung himself on science and philosophy.

The dichotomy between spiritual and animal essence, between ideal and bodily love, between moral determination and highly immoral reality, were played out by Kleist in his own substance. In the middle of August 1800 he made a secret journey. He wrote to Ulrike:

"I am now first seeking out a noble or wise friend with whom I can consult over the means to my end, since I feel too weak for it myself, although I was strong enough to determine the end itself irrevocably. Had you been a man — oh God, how fervently I have wished it! — Had you been a man — for a woman could not become my confidant — then I would not have had to seek this friend as far as I have now.

Do not guess at the purpose of my journey, even if you could. Remember that its achievement depends in part on secrecy from all, *all* men. For now at least. For one day it will by my pride and joy to tell it. Greet W. v. Z. She knows as much as you but not much more. — But send me through the post my paper on Kantian philosophy, in your possession, and also the cultural history which Auguste has; but at once.

I shall not be returning very soon, but you will keep all this to yourself. You shall know each time the place where I am; you will make no use of this confidence, which would obstruct the achievement of my purpose.

Be calm. Be quite calm. — Although a man's shell changes with every moon, one thing in him remains unchanging and eternal: *the feeling of his duty.*

Your faithful brother Heinrich

PS. Your commissions will be carried out tomorrow. — On all addresses to me you must always write that the letter will be collected personally."

Kleist always expressed himself mysteriously and enigmatically about the motives behind this journey. The friend he first asked was Brockes, a former classmate, whom Kleist described in a later letter to his fiancée as a "wonderful person". ("He studied in Göttingen, met love in Frankfurt-am-Main and it did not make him happy . . .") He wanted to travel with him to Vienna or Strasbourg in search of a cure for a malady of which we know only that Kleist thought it made him unfit for marriage. For pecuniary reasons, however, the friends only reached Würzburg and it turned out that the operation — for such it seems to have been — could be performed here. The demand made on the two girls they left behind them was almost presumptuous: they were to take Kleist at his word, honour his hidden purpose and thus earn his respect. So he required the unqualified consent of Ulrike and Wilhelmine, against all good sense and based on feeling alone. This is a subject of the first literary efforts which originated here, the *Familie Schroffenstein* and *Penthesilea*.

Kleist's life, what he thought and did, can only be discovered indirectly through his writing. He loved to play hide-and-seek and it would therefore be a mistake to sift through the statements he made on his journey as though a real secret were concealed in them and not simply Kleist's mystery-making. But if one takes a look at the pathological features displayed by Eros in the *Schroffensteins* and in *Penthesilea*, Kleist's passion for learning and obsession with scholarship can be interpreted as sublimations of something which was painful to him and connected with the animal aspects of existence: from where did Kleist get the objectivity for the assertions on his ego, that it was upright and faithful — if not from experience of intoxication and of urges in which this ego had once been dishonourable and unfaithful? Had he, like Brockes and with Brockes, met a love which did not make him happy, in Frankfurt as a young officer on the Rhine Campaign? For love must make people "happy"!?

In Würzburg Kleist recognized that literature was his future. He began to write here, no longer essays and diaries, but poetry. But we do not know *what* he wrote then. In this too he behaved secretively and expressed himself in subtle utterances, without revealing anything. Love was at the focus of his thinking; at home in Frankfurt were his fiancée and Ulrike, the two beloveds. The bipolarity of love, the physical phenomenon and the spiritual surrender, marriage and virginity, sultry sensuality and majestic purity, are the themes of this period. In *Schroffenstein* they are treated intensely in black and white, in *Penthesilea* majestically. Penthesilea has to realise that the body of her beloved cannot belong to her until the soul has fled from it. The fact that in marriage the body will also belong to the other person — this mingling which tortures all puritanically raised minds — was the very thing Kleist wanted to bring about in Würzburg. He wrote to Wilhelmine that after the journey he would be able to fulfil her "most sacred demands". Should one conclude from this that he was impotent or had venereal disease? The first possibility is excluded, since a man of 23 who wrote the sensual disrobing scene, the exchange of clothing, between the lovers and the confessions of the *Schroffenstein* family, must have been burning with sensual fires. Nor can these scenes be interpreted as the dreams of an overheated boyish imagination; Kleist was no late developer, he matured

Frankfurt an der Oder

early. All the stories and dramas contain great gallants who sought nothing but pleasure, from village judge Adam to Jupiter. It is quite possible that Kleist had been through a number of experiences on his campaigns and the journeyings of his early years. The crisis of his spirit may very well have come about through such experiences, which he describes in the novellas: a girl can be beautiful, lovable and charming and yet a trollop;

moral abandon can live within an appealing creature; at the moment of the greatest sensual intoxication one can acquire the seeds of a humiliating, even fatal disease. These are expressly Kleistian paradoxes. Love and knowledge, correlated terms in biblical language, are still identical for Kleist in the mystery of the *Amphitryon* drama. The lovers become known.

But one need not assume that Kleist's passion was of a painful nature. He loved exaggeration and concealment and it is much more likely that he was seeking a cure for a psychological inhibition which, of mental origin, affected the body. The profound horror of a virgin soul such as Penthesilea, faced with bodily love, is converted into a madness of love which brought the beloved to his death. Now he wrote to Wilhelmine:

"The inside of my soul looks like a philosopher's desk when he has thought up a new system and been writing down some of his main ideas on scattered bits of paper. A great idea — for you, Wilhelmine, hovers constantly before my mind . . . At that time I was not worthy of you, now I am. At that time I wept that you were so good, so noble, so estimable, so worthy of the highest happiness, now it will be my pride and my delight. At that time I was tormented by the knowledge that I could not fulfil your most sacred demands and now, now — But hush!

Now Wilhelmine, I too will tell you what I expect of the happiness of a future marriage. Before I dared not, but now — Oh God! How glad it makes me! I shall describe to you the wife who can *now* make me happy — and that is the great idea I have in mind for you . . . Fear not that the wife described will be no earthly one and that I shall find her only in heaven. I shall find her in five years' time on this earth and enfold her in my earthly arms."

At that time Kleist read the philosopher Immanuel Kant; he had already been concerned with him in Frankfurt-an-der-Oder. Yet the letters of these months reveal still more clearly the influence of another great author, Jean-Jacques Rousseau.

Students' winter costumes in Frankfurt an der Oder (water colour, 1805)

Parallel with his release from the popular philosophy of the Enlightenment and the ideal of scholarship (a practical application was to be to transmit the critical German philosophy to the French) was Kleist's discovery of feeling, emotion, the heart as the basic value of the soul. Rousseau became Kleist's authority for this. Curiously enough, since although Rousseau preaches Nature and Love, the pre-social state and perfect freedom of the ego, he built the ideal as a castle in the air. Kleist adopted the great idea naïvely and simply. Nature and Love became the vehicles of morality, the example was given by people in the loneliness of the mountains and their valleys; the natural man was good, the man in society was bad. State and Church, in *Earthquake in Chile*, were wicked; the rejects of society, Josephe and Jeronimo, were good. Rupert and Sylvester Schroffenstein, the representatives of the family, of convention, were bad; Ottokar and Agnes, who revolted against the law of their houses, were good. In the midst of the horror of annihilation they celebrate a paradisal love, just like Jeronimo and Josephe. Can the world be comprehended in this scheme?

This belief was bound to collapse rapidly, for Rousseau's theory rests on the unfulfillable presumption that there really is a naturally good, a "natural" human being. According to Rousseau, the fall of man comes about because he leaves nature when he establishes society and concludes the Contrat Social. In Emile's education, a rational motive, usefulness, takes the lead. Kleist still does not feel the contradiction; he emphatically adopts the human being who is by nature good, pure, noble and harmonious.

Kleist asks too much of his heroes and his fiancée, just as he did of books, from which he expected an elucidation of concepts. Harmonious man is made unhappy by social circumstances, by property and the corollary passions of envy, avarice and mistrust. These are the motifs of the dramatic apparatus in the *Schroffenstein* drama. *Käthchen von Heilbronn* — written much later but possibly already conceived then — contains the social motif of the noble, pure but poor maiden whom the count cannot marry until she has proved to be the emperor's daughter. It was the wrong track, but it was Kleist's, and from it arose the novellas *Earthquake* and *Foundling*. Both are stories of violation and lust which bring innocence low. Here a failure arose which is characteristic of Kleist's plays "in a very hidden way" (Muschg). It was only to be overcome in the form of the Doppelgänger, in a grotesquely comic manner in the Adam of the *Broken Jug*, with comic dignity in the Jupiter of *Amphitryon* and tragically in *Homburg*.

Kleist was cured in Würzburg and felt physically and spiritually sound. He wrote to Wilhelmine that it was *the most important day of our life.* He was freed from a nightmare, the tremendous tension between ignominy and beauty, animal and spiritual existence in man was — for an instant — lifted. His

30

letters became free, people and landscape were seen with different eyes and even in such secondary matters as finance the relief was obvious. Kleist had had to incur debts of 200 Thaler — yet, as he wrote to Ulrike, he would have paid ten times that amount.

By the end of October Kleist was back in Berlin, seeking permission from Minister Struensee to attend the meetings of the technical deputations; he wanted a position as a political economist in the Prussian Ministry of Economics, yet in November he is already complaining to his fiancée of the impossibility of his becoming a civil servant:

Heinrich von Kleist (copy of the original miniature of 1801)

"I am supposed to do what the State demands of me and yet I am not allowed to look into whether what it demands is good. I am supposed to be a mere tool for its unknown purposes — I cannot do it."

He suggested to his fiancée that she come and live with him and he would earn by teaching what they lacked for their maintenance. Was it a shame to give up the elegant way of life? Even Shakespeare was a groom and became the greatest poet of modern times! Kleist wanted to move with Wilhelmine to French Switzerland, where he could live by teaching German and where, he also believed, the French had a burning interest in the "newest philosophy", that of Kant.

He was asking too much of the general's daughter, with her conventional upbringing. Now, when Kleist suggested that she should live with him in modest circumstances, she took fright and could say neither yes nor no. Kleist returned to Berlin and buried himself in the study of Kant, until parallel letters of 22 and 23 March 1801 reached Wilhelmine and Ulrike — letters whose contents were bound to seem "terrible" to the ladies. To Wilhelmine he wrote:

"I recently became acquainted with the new Kantian philosophy, as it is called, and I must now tell you of an idea from it, while I do not fear that it will shake you as deeply and painfully as it has me. Nor do you know the whole sufficiently well to grasp its interest fully. I will put it as clearly as possible.

If everyone had green glass instead of eyes they would be bound to consider that the objects they saw through it were green — and they would never be able to decide whether their eyes were showing them things as they were or adding something to them which belonged, not to themselves but to the eyes. So it is with our understanding. We cannot decide whether what we call truth is truly truth, or whether it only seems so to us. If the latter, then the truth we are gathering here persists no longer after death — and all efforts to acquire something of one's own to follow us to the grave are vain.

Ah, Wilhelmine, if the point of this idea does not pierce your heart, then do not smile at another who feels himself wounded by it in his inmost being. My one, highest goal has sunk and now I have none."

"The city lies far below, as if in the midst of an amphitheatre . . ." (View of Würzburg)

Since Kleist believed that there was no truth to be found here below, he never touched a book; the ideal of knowledge had been destroyed, and more: the belief that this life had sense and meaning for the life beyond, and yet more: the core of cognition and with it the responsibility of the moral person.

Only a few years later, Wilhelmine von Zenge married Kant's insignificant successor in the Chair of Philosophy at Königsberg, Professor Krug. In a long letter she described to Krug her relationship with Heinrich von Kleist. She had not loved him. To begin with his brother Leopold had appealed to her more, for Heinrich "was very melancholy and gloomy and spoke very little". She had been taken by surprise when one evening, instead of the expected talk on the basic rules of the German language, which he had wanted to transmit to the ladies of Frankfurt society who spoke French better than German, Heinrich handed her a love letter. In the end she had yielded to his insistence and learned to treasure him. His ideals, his psychological grasp, which was admired even by the academic teachers, and his noble notion of morality fired her: she had tried to approximate to his ideal.

The World as Catastrophe

(The Schroffenstein Family)

His problems found their literary expression in *The Schroffenstein Family*, Kleist's first play. What he had read in Rousseau and Kant was his own problem; in both philosophers he had met a rational outline for what his own disillusionment with existence had been. The drama is incomparably more than a shell, than the dramatic garb of ideas, it is a poetic form. The blindness of the heads of both families, of whom one announced himself to be a murderer although he was not, is a reflection of Kleist's experience that reality always deceives us as to the true character of existence. All the characters are deceived, so that ultimately the fathers kill their own children.

Kant, like Kleist, sought certainty of cognition. Kant had asked what means of cognition would have to exist in us and in what manner and connection they would have to work, in order that, for instance, mathematical cognition, the law of causality, practical experience and the axioms of the observation of nature should possess undoubted validity. Kant was no radical revolutionary, doubting all principles; he was investigating the assumptions of our experience, not the legitimacy of cognition in general. Kant never dealt with the problem of error and its possibility. His doctrines, like the sensualism and rationalism of the enlightened century — which was also the basis of Kleist's education — circle round the relationships of the psychological powers to one another. Mathematics are possible because they gives cognitions of such a general and necessary nature that they cannot proceed from experience.

What Kleist probably did not rightly understand in Kant was the heuristic character of the category of "as if" introduced by Kant; he did not follow the Kantian road to its end, where it justifies the experience of reality by new means. He remained at a point of understanding which suited the tenor of his own life, namely the obscurity, uncertainty and ambiguity of all phenomena on the one hand and the deceptive character of our reason and of feelings on the other. Whom may one trust: oneself, one's nearest and dearest, feeling, cognition? It is in no sense true that Kant was the first to open his eyes. Only a few weeks later he wrote almost mockingly of the confusion into which the Kantian philosophy had thrown him in March 1801. So it was not Kant's philosophy which shook him, but the formulation he found there for his own experience — or what he held it to be. The experience is to be found in *The Schroffenstein Family*.

The play was first called *Die Familie Ghonorez* and set in Spain. L. Wieland advised him to transfer the action to Germany and to set the time somewhere in the then "modern" chivalric Middle Ages. Two lines in the same family have a mutual contract of inheritance which has spoiled the atmosphere. They suspect one another of the foul murder of each other's children. True, the murderers' confessions were elicited on the rack; true, no one knew anything definite, yet even the benevolent among the family were forced to assume that all evil came from the other related line, which was planning the destruction of their own. Imagination is stronger than truth, appearance stronger than reality. So the play begins with a blasphemous oath by the Rossitz Schroffensteins to take bloody revenge for the presumed murder of the Warwand Schroffensteins. Jeronimus, trying to mediate, himself becomes the victim of an assault: the honourable peacemaker is regarded as a villain hired by the opposition. The action hastens to its end with fearful parallelism. With Agnes from the Warwand house and Ottokar from the Rossitz house, who love each other, incognito, the feud between the lines seems to have been overcome. Yet, lying in ambush for the child of the enemy, each father stabs his own, for Agnes and Ottokar have exchanged clothes. The reconciliation over the bodies of the lovers comes too late.

Paris and Switzerland

(Robert Guiskard)

Kleist took the *Schroffenstein Family* with him when he set out on his first journey abroad. Besides the sketches of *Käthchen* and *Penthesilea,* among his novellas and play drafts was a Norman play for which he wanted to undertake some historical study in Paris. The love scenes of the *Schroffenstein Family* were probably first written in Paris. After Wieland and Schiller, Kleist had by now been absorbed in reading, in fact studying, the most important author in German literature: Goethe. *Hermann und Dorothea* had been published in 1797. Here the theme of the conquest of temporal needs by love had been convincingly carried through.

Kleist wanted to leave Berlin; in the technical department of the Ministry, under its Director Kuhnt, he had been irritated by the pedantic pace of business and terrorised by the service. When one day his superior told him to read a multi-volume technical and scientific work and report on it, he decided to leave the Ministry. For what, he did not know. Ulrike was to bring money, he obtained himself a passport and to the officials' question as to the purpose of his journey he said that he must finish his studies of chemistry and physics in Paris, the capital of that discipline. That nothing much could come of such studies was clear; it was one of the reasons why Kleist was later hesitant about going to Berlin, because he had proclaimed all too loudly that his studies were pressing and given people to understand that he would return as a scholar.

In April 1801 he left with Ulrike; their first stop was Leipzig. At the beginning of May they were in Dresden, where Kleist astounded an art expert by his mature and well-considered judgements of works of art. He envied the young artists of the Academy and was pleased to hear that Wouwerman, for whom he had an unusual liking, had not become an artist until his forties.

In Dresden he received a lasting impression of the Catholic world which he had still been mocking in Würzburg. Hearing church music inspired him to write the story *St. Cecila or the Power of Music*. Although some anti-clerical features may still appear in *The Foundling* and *The Earthquake,* it is now the iconoclasts who are restrained from their misdeeds by the power of music and atone with madness for their blasphemous plan to desecrate the church.

Brother and sister drove in their own carriage with a coachman and two retired Polish Hussar horses bought for the purpose. Ulrike wore men's clothing and not only for practical reasons. She was an androgynous type. They reached the Rhine via Göttingen and made an excursion by ship to Cologne from

Mainz. They arrived in Paris, via Mannheim and Strasbourg, at the beginning of July, in time for the commemoration of the great revolution. From the first moment, Kleist disliked the great metropolis. He found it stale, vapid and overpopulated, so that one forgot people as soon as they turned the corner. He called its inhabitants too gracefully knowing to be true. Wilhelm von Humboldt was the right man to introduce the young Prussian into the scientific world, but Kleist complained: "the people talk to me of alkalis and acids while an almighty need parches my lips".

"Oh, I cannot describe to you the impression made on me by the first sight of this highest immorality allied to the highest science. Whither will the fate of this nation lead? God knows. It is riper for downfall than any other European nation. Sometimes, when I look at the libraries where the works of Rousseau, Helvétius and Voltaire, stand in splendid rooms and splendid volumes, I think, what use have they been? Has one of them achieved its goal? Have they succeeded in holding back

Dresden. View of the old city across the Elbe
(Painting by Kuehl, section)

"The withered oak, stands unshaken in the storm . . ."
("Krähenhorst an der Küste Rügens". Painting by Caspar David Friedrich,
USA, private ownership)

the wheel which hurries ineluctably on, hurtling towards its
own abyss? Oh, if only all those who have *written* good works
had *done* the half of that good, the world would be a better
place! Even this study of nature itself, on which the whole mind
of the French nation has fallen with almost its united strength,
where will it lead? Why does the State waste millions on all
these institutes for the propagation of scholarship? Is it concerned with *truth?* The *State?* A state knows no other advantage
than the one it can calculate in percentages. It wants to *use* the
truth — and for what? For arts and crafts. It wants to make the
comfortable still more comfortable, to sensualize the sensual, to
refine still more the most refined of luxuries. And if, at the end,
even the most voluptuous and pampered want can formulate no

further wish, what then —? Oh, how incomprehensible is the will which reigns over the human race! Without science we quake before every celestial phenomenon, our life is vulnerable to every beast of prey, a poisonous plant can kill us — and as soon as we step into the kingdom of knowledge, as soon as we use our learning to secure and protect ourselves, the first step has been taken towards luxury, and with it all the vices of sensuality . . ."

This is Kleist's critique of civilization; two generations before Nietzsche and Burckhardt, he has assambled all the arguments of the European decay.

The ideal he had in his head was inevitably pushed aside by Paris. On 16 August 1801 he reached the point of a real atrocity letter about Paris. As the two fortresses stand in hostile opposition to each other in the *Schroffenstein Family,* the pairs of lovers oscillating between them as messengers in No Man's Land, so Kleist's world fell apart. It is one of the greatest riddles that at such an early age he was able to live so unreservedly in a world of his own, weaving and unravelling the plots! Passages of letters from Paris show that the poet's personality had found its symbols and subjects. There are sentences which are taken up again almost word for word, years later, in *Penthesilea* and *Hermannsschlacht:* "The withered oak stands unshaken in the storm, which overthrows the tree in bloom because it can grip it by the crown." "I do not understand how a poet can hand over the child of his love to such a crude rabble as men are." "Among the Persian magi there was a religious law: a man could do nothing more pleasing to God than this: to work a field, to plant a tree and to conceive a child. — I call that wisdom and no truth has yet pierced so deep into my soul as this." In Paris the letters suddenly take on their unmistakable note. Even when they touch on secondary things, it is Heinrich von Kleist speaking. In Rousseau's formula that town was bad, country good, Kleist found his own justification for leaving Paris. An idyll of the lovers who hold one another closely

Ball on 14 July 1801, in celebration of the storming of the Bastille

embraced in the midst of the turmoil of popular merrymaking may have become the core of Ottokar's love scene with Agnes — it was also taken for the *Betrothal in San Domingo*, the first version of which was set against the background of the French Revolution. The scenes are caves and gardens, lonely houses and closed rooms, to which man has fled from the world.

As late as 1828, Ulrike von Kleist was recounting from memory: "We had intended to spend a year in Paris, but the whole French way of life appealed so little to Heinrich that he could not endure for more than four months and then went to Switzerland, where he settled on a lonely little island near Thun in the Aare to work out his *Schroffenstein Family*. I returned to Frankfurt." Ulrike had no reason to mention that she had quarrelled seriously with Heinrich. Their close proximity had done neither of them good; Kleist had recognised what a problematic character his half-sister was. Ulrike von Kleist was

41

an intellectual type, wanting in feminine spontaneity of heart. Even in Paris she wore men's clothing and it was said that only a blind flautist had perceived her sex and called her Madame. Kleist made his complaint to Wilhelmine: "Oh, there is no being in the world whom I honour as I do my sister. But what a blunder nature made when she formed a being which was neither man nor woman and wavers like an amphibian between two species! The conflict between will and strength is striking in this creature." She was a virago who had "forgotten" her sex. Ulrike's character gave Kleist his first idea for *Penthesilea*. Now he tried tactfully to unburden himself of her presence, but he failed and this created a tension which did not slacken until Ulrike left.

Meanwhile Kleist had again proposed to his fiancée in Frankfurt that she should come to him and live with him as a farmer's wife in Switzerland. A few weeks later, shortly before Kleist's departure from Paris, came the negative reply. Wilhelmine's argument was cogent: she did not feel physically up to the strenuous life of a farmer. Kleist tried yet again to persuade her, in vain. He travelled to Switzerland while Ulrike returned to relations in Frankfurt. She was received uncomfortably. What had become of Heinrich's studies in Paris? Why had he let her travel across half Europe alone? What was the meaning of this ridiculous idea about agriculture? The von Zenge family no longer had any faith in Wilhelmine's fiancé either: how could he want to make a farmer's wife of a general's daughter? These very human arguments were accompanied by ones of fortune. The trip to Paris had greatly reduced Heinrich's share of the property. Nevertheless Kleist complained that the money had been badly managed, even talking of deception by his relations and demanding that Ulrike relinquish all financial ties with the family by paying off his debts. He angrily rejected curt commands to come home.

Kleist was sick. He was suffering from headaches and feelings of apprehension. He wandered restlessly about in Switzerland, looking at farms which were for sale. Finally he settled on

Kleist's cottage on the island of Delosea, Lake Thun

"I am now living on an island in the Aare where it leaves Lake Thun, quite surrounded by Alps, nearly 2 kilometres from the town. I have rented for 6 months a little cottage on the tip, which was very cheap owing to its isolation. I live in it all alone."

Kleist to his sister Ulrike, 1 May 1802

that lonely island near Thun in the Aare; a friendly fisherman's family supplied him with necessities. Here he finished writing the *Schroffensteins* and pondered the draft of *Guiskard.*

William of Normandy, founder of the Norman State in Italy, had three brothers who succeeded one another in government. Abelard, son of the third, did not come to power because his guardian, Robert Guiscard, William's fourth son, assumed power and reigned for thirty years. He managed to get his own son Robert accepted as the heir to the throne. His daughter Helena was the widowed Empress of Byzantium and the bride of Abelard, the pretender to the throne usurped by Robert. This is the historical basis of the play as set down by Kleist in the footnotes. The source of *Guiskard* was a paper in Schiller's journal *Die Horen* of 1797. Kleist may have gained his inspiration for the subject from Goethe's *Wilhelm Meister,* where there is a reference to Tancred. In Paris he then read the *Denkwürdigkeiten aus dem Leben des griechischen Kaisers Alexius* (Memorabilia from the life of the Greek Emperor Alexius), by his daughter Anna Comnena.

Robert Guiscard was besieging Byzantium; plague was raging through his army. The hero, with his strapping physique, bore the seeds of the deadly disease within him. The subject of the connection between the spiritual and animal nature of man, glorious appearance and fatally sick reality, is exalted and poeticised here: the strong man rules the world in the form of Guiscard, while the legitimate representative of authority, Abelard, works away without comparable glamour in the background. What in the *Schroffensteins* was a dense tangle of deception, evil, mistrust, confusion, violence and error, is summoned up in *Robert Guiskard* in ten scenes of fifteen pages. The play remained a fragment. Kleist appears to have destroyed two copies in despair. The whole, if it ever existed, would in fact be the unification of antique greatness with Shakespeare, as Wieland commented. Probably no complete play ever existed, since the fragment available exhausts the problem. Guiscard's character did not need further expansion,

"Le Juge ou la cruche cassée"
(Engraving by J. J. Le Veau after a painting by Ph. Debucourt, section)

because it is enclosed within itself. In Kleist the suffering hero can only be a woman: Käthchen, Evchen, Liesbeth Kohlhaas, Alkmene. The active woman, who tries to reverse the laws of nature, Penthesilea, comes to grief.

The superior, the lofty human being, even when marked by a fatal illness, knows that the world is a paradox and morally inconsistent. If Kant destroyed the naive realism of the young Kleist, his disillusionment found its symbol in Guiscard.

On closer examination, *Robert Guiskard* does have its faults. They lie in the poet's relationship to the characters. In the original draft the disinherited Abelard attracted Kleist's interest, whereas Guiscard was more of a tyrant — as were all Kleistian princes up to Hermann.

The subject of hatred of tyrants was exemplified by Kleist as Napoleon, the "Consul of the World" in his letters of 2 and 18 March 1802. The French usurper was then menacing Switzerland and Kleist saw his agricultural idyll directly threatened. But at that time he did not hate Napoleon — as he did later —

45

for political and patriotic reasons; his reasons were idealistic. Napoleon was the tyrant corrupting the freedom of the people. Kleist was at that time entertaining the idea of a play on Leopold, in which he would magnify the struggle of the free Swiss against a power-hungry tyrant, Duke Leopold III of Austria. For unknown reasons the material was abandoned in favour of another: Peter the Hermit, the "General in Monk's Habit". Peter started a crusade from religious fanaticism and thereby invoked the "dehumanisation of Europe". Thus *Peter the Hermit* is seen to have stirred up the anti-clerical movement. When this plan too was abandoned, Kleist returned to Guiscard and planted features of anti-despotism in his Guiscard character. The despotic features were not expunged until the fragment was published in *Phöbus*, 1808. By then Kleist had overcome Rousseau and developed into an aristocrat.

Unfortunately we do not know how many scenes there were of *Guiskard*, which of them were burned in Paris and which Kleist kept in writing, or in his head. The reason for their destruction is clear: the author did not like them. Just as he asked his family not to read *Schroffenstein* because the play did not satisfy his demands, so Kleist regarded *Guiskard* as a failure and destroyed it. The guilty party is Rousseau, who explained all conflict externally, from social prejudice. For years he prevented Kleist from recognising that for him it was a question of inner truth, of spiritual responsibility. It was not until 1807—1808, in Dresden, that Kleist wrote down the surviving fragment.

The Satirical Record

(The Broken Jug)

There is a youthful poem of Kleist's in two versions, the *Jünglingsklage* (Lament of Youth), of which the second runs:

> "Winter retreating
> grizzled and dear,
> stilled all our feeling
> to ice, hard and clear.
> Now under Springtime's
> exuberant breath
> the streams are all thawing,
> and you too, my breast!"

What winter's passing is lamented here and what exuberant spring does the poet fear? Like almost all Kleist's work, this poem also conceals more than it reveals. One finds in it a universality of judgement, the youth's feeling played out through the motif of the contrasting seasons, through the imagery of which the mysterious sensual torment of boyhood glimmers. Kleist feared lust because he feared its paramountcy, and begs winter to still his feelings into ice. In his utterances on love we find an astounding realism which is converted at a certain level into pure lasciviousness, in the person of the village judge Adam in *The Broken Jug,* who likes getting in with pretty girls at night, whereas on another level it is the extreme of gallantry, in the person of Jupiter approaching Alkmene in *Amphitryon.*

Love, in particular, contains a dialectical 'for' and 'against'; it is love which shows human beings in the entanglement of spiritual and physical, of the psyche and the body. So we have on the one hand the efforts of Adam to taste the most primitive side of love, physical possession, and on the other side stands

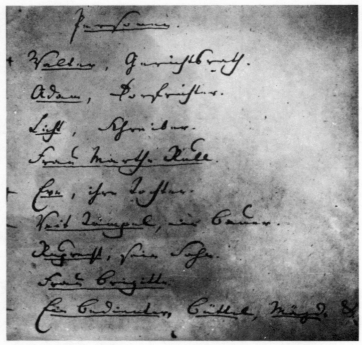

Cast list from Kleist's copy of "Der Zerbrochene Krug".

Evchen, the sweet creature whose very existence lies in the preservation of what Adam would like to steal like a thief in the night. Appearances are against Evchen and the guilty judge Adam encourages the world of this false appearance and thereby commits his crime: the false attribution of guilt to the innocent. One should not try to mould Adam and Eve on the basis of their names, as though Kleist's *Broken Jug* were a crypto-drama on the fall of the first man. Insofar as the biblical Fall is a basic model for temptation and guilt, Kleist has merely hit on an eternal pattern for humanity. Whereas elsewhere he approaches his plots gravely, almost ceremoniously and as if in rage, here he is behaving in an easy-going, even idyllic manner. The milieu is a windless area, the Dutch countryside. Kleist

48

enjoys the scenes with the guilty judge as a burlesque entanglement in a web of brilliant lies. This is a virtuoso performance and the fact that he could do it displays Kleist's technical genius in the dramatic field. Yet this is not the core of the matter.

The language betrays that this is not a case of a great artist

Emil Jannings as the village judge Adam in the Ufa film "Der Zerbrochene Krug", based on Kleist's text

showing off his talents in farce, for once, because it amuses him. The play stands in relation to Kleist's basic problem of how man becomes and remains sure of himself, transcending the enigmatic character of the world. He called it the *imperturbability of feeling* which is the last resort of the ego. As Kleist's foreword says, the play originated from seeing an engraving of a court scene in the Dutch manner. The scene is attested for 1802 in Switzerland by Zschokke. The play was slowly prepared during Kleist's journeys but not finished until 1805/6 in Königsberg. Chronologically it is linked with *Guiskard* and *Amphitryon*. The comedy is a satirical record of a court scene where they are trying to discover the truth, the victory of truth over appearances, against probability. The thorny central point of the proceedings is the innocence of the girl, immaculacy as the fundamental state of the *gracious creature*. But the hero is not the woman but the tempter, the liar, who would himself so much like to apply to the devil in explanation of wickedness, Adam the village judge — that can only be a comic hero.

The *Broken Jug* is not based on an idea but on a scene, and its execution is the real content of the comedy — with ideas glinting through here and there.

In this play Kleist pushed the cat-and-mouse game with the details of villainy to its most extreme, in wit, in innuendo, ambiguity, deliberate or foolish misunderstanding, talking at cross purposes, attribution of false statements, opinions and facts, the persuasion of wrong, the art of distortion. Walter, the court counsel who has come to study the peculiar practices of this court's procedure, and by no means to improve them, enters into it. He builds golden bridges for Adam and only at the last moment do the State, the law and bureaucracy give place to truth in his mouth.

In the fire of Kleist's searing humour the villain becomes almost a sympathetic human being. His self-obsession and lechery do not appear as moral vices but as the weaknesses of a vital nature. A peculiar sympathy transfigures the abuse of office and dignity. Adam boozes, gobbles, whores, lies and regards the whole world as gullible and credulous, just as every girl is an object of his lust. He believes so firmly in the external trappings of the office, the position, the social consideration, the legal convention, and in his own words and lies, that they have an implicit innocence and seem like the foolishness of a Falstaff or a Don Quixote. He is rooted in lies. He is quite incapable by now of belief in truth and goodness, even where it could be of use to him in an emergency. He is the perfect picture of a world ruined by bureaucracy which regards its blindness as a stage of extreme enlightenment. The world is diminished, but in the diminished relationships it comes right again. Adam talks uninterruptedly and the more he talks, to talk himself out of it, the more suspect does the content of his speech become. He does not tie himself in knots dialectically, he is too cunning for that, but his tirading art leads him into the details of that confusion which lies at the bottom of the world. By talking, Adam contrives to miss the real point of his speech, the truth. His happiness is that of impudence and sometimes one seems to sense how sad Kleist was that the happiness of feasting, boozing and whoring was denied to him. Adam lives in a paradise of the most barefaced naiveté and enjoyment.

Kleist, who was always in search of paradise, whether as a "scholar" or as a traveller on his journeys through half Europe, or in the dreams of a Swiss agricultural idyll, had the world of judge Adam behind him since Kant. But where was his pride now? He had reflected it most symbolically in his girls and women, those gracious creatures. They were the pure vessels of his concepts of love and history: Eve and Käthchen, Alkmene and Penthesilea. They are so many enhancements and exaggerations of the concept of "Love", as most of the love poetry of our literature has remained fixed in the fate of Gretchen. For Kleist's girls and women it is not a matter of private or married happiness or unhappiness, but of verification and confirmation, of confidence in the origin and feeling of the high, impregnable vocation. Lovers give themselves up and hand themselves over, to earn a real existence. The dying Toni in *Betrothal in San*

51

Illustration to "Der Zerbrochene Krug" by Adolph Menzel

Domingo complains that she should have been trusted, and the humble Eve of the *Broken Jug* protests against making admissions to the tribunal which do not concern it. She possesses a secret of which Adam knows only the word: Love.

Eve talks coherently, descriptively, she does not fall in with the staccato of the men with their cunning operations. In her speech the verse becomes melodious, almost emphatic. She does not use speech as an instrument for something, but as the sound, like music, of a truth which has only to be heard in order to be there. It ist extraordinary that Goethe had no ear for this when he had the *Broken Jug* performed, inadequately, in Weimar. Classical Weimar could have no understanding and could not even produce a laugh, for the new man caricatured in Adam and symbolically represented in Eve.

Kleist's Odyssey

Ulrike had been back in Frankfurt for barely a month or two when Karl Wilhelm von Pannwitz, Lord of Babow and Gulben, the brother of Kleist's dead mother, received a letter from Bern from his nephew Heinrich von Kleist saying that he was sick and in need of money. The letter sounded alarming. In case he had died meanwhile, the money was to be sent to the doctor and apothecary Karl Wyttenbach in Bern. Ulrike, only recently dismissed by her brother, lent money at once, put on her men's clothing and travelled night and day by post horses to Switzerland. There civil order was in chaos, Napoleon's troops were on the march; Ulrike tried to get into the town but General Erlach was encamped before Bern with an army corps. She succeeded in penetrating the military cordon and reaching the town. There she sought out the doctor and asked after her brother: he was well, she learned, and she betook herself to his place. Heinrich clasped his hands to his head: "Ulrike, what is this? You really

look as if you had just gone out of the door and come in again."
(She was wearing the same travelling clothes in which she had
left him so few months before and this looking-just-the-same
was what preoccuppied him most in the first few moments.)
Kleist was well again. He had even promised some young
friends of his that he would help them to defend the town if
General Erlach came. With pain and toil Ulrike succeeded in
dissuading him from this plan.

In the next few days, when the political excitement had died
down, Kleist showed his sister his Aare island and introduced
her to his friends. These were the bookseller Heinrich Gessner,
a son of the idyll writer, Heinrich Zschokke from Magdeburg
who had been living in Switzerland for a long time and Ludwig
Wieland, son of the famous father. The young Wieland, "a
restless mind with a satirical tongue", had taken a position with
the old Bernese government and was now expressing himself so
incautiously about the French and Francophiles that it was
thought advisable for him to leave the town in haste. Heinrich
suggested that Ulrike should actively support the penniless
refugee. There was already an industrious police force at his
heels. Wieland, for his part, was grateful. He invited Kleist to
travel with him to his father.

Kleist had already met the elder Wieland as an ensign and
reverred him. The young Wieland had sent his father some of
his friends' manuscripts, probably the *Familie Schroffenstein*,
and Wieland had taken a liking to Kleist. If he wanted to be a
poet, Wieland could help him. As Editor of the *Teutscher
Merkur* and through his connections with Herder and Goethe
he was one of the key figures of literary life. In the social
structure of German literature at that time, with the almost
unbounded predominance of Goethe and Schiller and the value
of Goethe's judgement among those who counted, it might be
useful to Kleist — quite apart from reasons of deep respect — to
meet the greatest poet of the nation face to face and talk to him.
Moreover, Goethe was Director of the most important German
theatre, the Weimar Hoftheater.

What happened next cannot be explained. Apparently the young Wieland played a dirty trick on Kleist by stopping in Erfurt and instead of taking Kleist to his father, remaining in the arms of a youthful love. Kleist went to Weimar alone.

A year and a half later, Christoff Martin Wieland wrote to Dr. Wedekind in Mainz, who was treating Kleist. He said that Kleist, who was living in Weimar, had visited him twice on his estate at Ossmannstedt. He had found him tense but personally extremely likeable and therefore, in accordance with his nature, he had been warm and open with the young poet — but Kleist had been reserved. Something mysterious and enigmatic, which seemed to lie deeper than anything which a connoisseur of men such as Wieland might have thought affected, made Kleist hold off at an awkward distance. But when, shortly after, Wieland heard from his son that Kleist was living in a wretched quarter of Weimar and would gratefully accept an invitation to Ossmannstedt, he did not hesitate to invite Kleist to his home and Kleist decided "despite a very pretty daughter of Wieland's", as he wrote to Ulrike, to accept the invitation in January 1803. He stayed as a guest within the Wieland family for some ten weeks.

Of course, there were reasons for Wieland to find his guest remarkable. Kleist often seemed distrait; for instance, a single word seemed to bring into his head a whole series of ideas, "like a glockenspiel" with the result that he heard nothing more that was said to him and so failed to respond. Another peculiarity which seemed to his host to verge on madness was that at table Kleist frequently spoke between his teeth, as if to himself; but Kleist admitted that at such moments of absentmindedness he was preoccupied with his play. It had been in his mind for a long time, but he had not succeeded in getting it onto paper as a whole. Wieland continues: "I then took all possible pains to move him to execute his play according to the plan he had drawn up and to finish it as well as it could be done and then to let me know so that I could give him my opinion of it; or if he did not want that, at least to complete it for himself, in order that he could review in better... Finally, after many vain efforts and pleas to be shown just a single scene of this fatal work of his destiny, one day by chance in the afternoon the happy moment came when I succeeded in making him confident enough to declaim to me some of the essential scenes and several fragments of others from memory (!). I declare that I was astonished and I think I shall not be saying too much if I assure you that if the spirits of Aeschylus, Sophocles and Shakespeare united to create a tragedy, that would be Kleist's Death of Guiscard the Norman, insofar as the whole corresponds to what he has let me hear. From that moment on it was decided that Kleist was born to fill the great gap in our literature which, in my opinion at least, has not yet been filled even by Schiller and Goethe."

Kleist was 25, Luise Wieland only 13. She was sick with love for Kleist. He wrote to Ulrike: "I have found more love than is right and sooner or later I must go away; my curious fate!" Wieland is supposed to have thought of making Kleist his son-in-law, but Kleist left and gave no further sign of life to either father or son. Oscillating between genius and madness, as if driven by furies, he could not find peace. On departure he confided to Wieland a plan to apprentice himself to a cabinet-maker in Koblenz. He wanted to strangle his genius in order to avoid the temptation to suicide. Was he an "inexpressible human being"? He himself did not know why he had to leave a house "where I have found more love than the whole world together can produce, apart from you! But I had to go. Oh heaven, what kind of world is this!" he wrote to Ulrike.

"I spent the next few days in an inn in Weimar and did not know where to turn ... Finally I decided to go to Leipzig ... I am receiving instruction here in declamation from one Kerndörffer. I am learning to declaim my own tragedy with him. Well declaimed, it must make a better impression than badly presented. Performed with perfect declamation it would make a quite unusual effect. When I read it aloud to old Wieland with great fire (!), I so succeeded in inflaming him that I lost the

Christoph Martin Wieland (Painting by Jagemann)

Ernst von Pfuel (1779—1866), Kleist's friend, in old age (photograph)

power of speech for joy at his inner excitement and flung myself at his feet, showering his hands with hot kisses.

The day before yesterday I took heart and went to Hindenburg[1]. There was great joy. 'Well, how are mathematics in Paris?' A silly answer from me and a sorrowful look at the ground from his side. — 'So you've just been travelling around?' — 'Yes, travelling around.' He shook his head dolefully. Finally I gave him to understand that I actually was working at *something*. 'Then what is it you're working at? Now! Aren't I allowed to know? You spent this winter with Wieland; certainly! certainly!' — And then I fell on his neck and hugged and kissed him until he laughingly agreed with me that a man must extend the talent in which he feels himself to be preeminent."

The public began to notice the new poet. Wieland had recommended Kleist to Göschen, the publisher, who printed the *Schroffenstein Family*. Now a newspaper article appeared in the "Freimüthiger": *The Appearance of a new Poet*[2]. Kleist recommended Ulrike to read it without saying why — but in the same letter he asked her not to read the play praised in it. If he could be allowed to work at home in Frankfurt for a few months without driving him mad with anxiety as to what was to become of him, he would, he wrote, *roll* with joy in the parlour.

In Dresden Kleist met Pfuel, in addition to his old friends. When Pfuel questioned his talent as a comic writer, Kleist read him *The Broken Jug*. Pfuel was struck by it and further confirmed Kleist in his belief in his talent. They must have been strange weeks and months: Kleist, tearing himself to pieces over the final form of *Guiskard,* full on the one hand of proud exaltation and the threat that he was going to snatch the laurels

[1] Professor of Mathematics in Leipzig whom Kleist had met in May 1801 when he was visiting the learned world of Göttingen and Leipzig.

[2] Jean Paul was so struck with the *Schroffenstein Family* that in his *Vorschule der Ästhetik* which appeared in 1804 he referred to this play alongside works by Novalis, Zacharias Werner and Clemens Brentano as an example of young literature.

of the greatest German writer from Goethe's head, and on the other hand tempted to suicide by the non-success of *Guiskard,* had to be laboriously soothed. Pfuel tried to distract him from his suicidal intentions by mockery, at which Kleist, good-humoured by nature, would laugh. But when he repeatedly continued to suggest to Pfuel that they die together, Pfuel proposed a joint journey to Switzerland or France as a cure. Kleist agreed to his proposal. Once again a passionate love-story seems to have hastened his departure. He was on friendly terms with the von Schlieben family, whose eldest daughter Karoline was the fiancée of his friend Lohse, the painter, who was at that time studying in Switzerland. The second daughter, Henriette, had set Kleist alight; there may even have been an over-hasty betrothal. Henriette gave him an embroidered half-shirt as a parting gift. The girls were so poor that, as Kleist only now discovered, they sold their own handwork.

Pfuel and Kleist travelled on foot, lacking the money for a carriage, horses and coachman. The surviving letters sound half sinisterly, half joyously tense. Forced to ask Ulrike for money, he wrote on 3 July 1803:

"So I ask of you, my dear one, as much respite for my life as I shall need to satisfy in full its great intention. You will readily help me to the single delight which awaits me, however belatedly, in my future, I mean, to weave for me the wreath of immortality. Your friend, Art and the world will one day thank you for it."

Kleist knew that his destiny was approaching its crisis. In his baggage he was carrying *Guiskard* and *Penthesilea,* both unfinished and from both he hoped for a happy outcome to his crisis; the completion "of the poem", of *his* poem, would be happiness.

The friends walked to Bern and Thun. In Meyringen they met the Werdecks from Potsdam, in Varese, Lohse the painter; They reached Milan via Bellinzona, walked back through Vaud and finally reached Paris via Geneva and Lyons. Here they met the Werdecks again. On 5 October, in Geneva, Kleist wrote perhaps the most famous of his letters to Ulrike:

"Heaven knows, my dearest Ulrike, (and may I die if it is not literally true), how gladly I would give a drop of my heart's blood for every letter of a letter which could begin: 'My poem is finished'. But you know who, according to the saying, does more than he can. I have now used up half a thousand successive days, including the nights of most of them, in the attempt to bring down yet another wreath to add to the many of our family: now our divine guardian goddess has called to me that it is enough. Touched, she kisses the perspiration from my brow and comforts me. 'If every one of her dear sons would do as much there would be a place for our name among the stars.' So let it be enough. Fate, which measures out every addition to the civilisation of nations, does not, I think, yet wish art to mature under these northern skies. At least it would be foolish if I were any longer to expend my powers on a work which, as I must at last persuade myself, is too hard for me. I yield to One who is not yet there and, a millennium too soon, I bow before his

Kleist's friends Henriette and Karoline von Schlieben

spirit. For in the series of human inventions the one I have conceived is undoubtedly a component part, and somewhere a stone is already growing for the one who first expresses it.

Then am I never to be allowed to return to you, my dearest people? Oh never! Do not persuade me. If you do, then you do not know the dangerous thing that is called ambition. I can laugh about it now, when I think of myself as a pretender with claims among a crowd of people who do not recognise their birthright to the crown; but the consequences for a sensitive mind are, I swear to you, incalculable. The idea appals me.

But is it not unworthy of fate to condescend to lead such a helpless thing as man by the nose? And am I not entitled to call it that, when it so to speak hands us out shares in goldmines which, when we begin to dig, contain no precious metal at all? Hell gave me my half-talents, heaven gives a man a whole one, or none at all.

I cannot tell you how great my suffering is. I would wish with all my heart to go where no man can ever go! A certain unjust bitterness against it has overcome me . . . Farewell, greet everyone — I can do no more.

Heinrich."

A fortnight later the manuscript of *Guiskard* was burned in Paris and probably also the drafts of the Leopold and Peter play. Then he left Paris, alone, on foot, without a passport, heading for Boulogne-sur-Mer. On the way he wrote from St. Omer to Ulrike on 26 October saying that he sought death, since heaven had denied him fame, the greatest good on earth: "I shall die the splendid death of battle . . . shall take service with the French, the army will soon be rowing over to England, the ruin of all of us lies in wait across the seas, I rejoice at the prospect of the eternally lovely grave."

The crisis had come. What Kleist did was madness, an heroically veiled suicide, also politically ambiguous, for what was a Prussian officer doing in Napoleon's army? The act gave rise to a mistrust of Kleist by the Prussian king and Government. It was in fact frivolous, for a Prussian guards officer travelling to France without a passport could, if he were arrested, at once be shot as a spy. So it was fortunate that shortly before Boulogne an acquaintance, an army doctor, happened on the wandering poet and forced him to apply at once to Lucchesini, the Ambassador in Paris, for a pass; only recently a Prussian nobleman had been shot as a supposed spy of the Russian Tsar.

Kleist followed the suggestion, returned to Paris, and Lucchesini made him out a pass for Potsdam — which forced Kleist to go home. On this journey he was afflicted in the Rhineland by a violent — unknown — illness, of which that same Hofrat Wedekind from whom Wieland had received news of Kleist, could not cure him for months [1]. The world did not hear of him, but he seems to have made the acquaintance of one Karoline von Günderode and to have had a tender relationship with the daughter of a preacher in Wiesbaden. Then suddenly "this enchanting Kleist" appeared at Wieland's house in Weimar. Eight years later Luise Wieland wrote of this visit to her sister: "Still just the same lovable person who was so interesting on account of his spirit, and over and above that, his still very modest, quiet character and behaviour. My father greeted him as an old friend and I with a control which I had painstakingly assumed. So I maintained myself in this mode, even when I was alone with him, until his departure a few days later."

Kleist went to Potsdam. Pfuel was stationed there with his regiment and thought he was seeing a ghost when one evening, when he was already in bed, Kleist appeared in his room. The friendship was soon restored and they wondered what the returning wanderer was to do in Prussia. He went to Berlin and

---

[1] To his Dresden friend Henriette von Schlieben, Kleist wrote a year later from Berlin: "I am not able to give reasonable people any insight into this extraordinary journey. I myself have lost any understanding of its motive since my illness and no longer comprehend how certain things could have succeeded on one another."

The French Guard on parade before Napoleon I in the Berlin recreation grounds, October 1806

sought an audience at court, but the king was in Charlottenburg and there Kleist managed to have an interview with Adjutant-General von Köckeritz. He referred to a report which Lucchesini must have sent to the king, his own testimonials, which must have borne all the features of mental illness — and could he now hope not to be hauled before a "political court"? He felt restored and would like to apply to the king for an appointment.

Köckeritz, the typical royal aide, was no more than reflecting the mood of court society with regard to Kleist when he responded negatively, with the question as to whether Kleist was really quite restored and whether, and above all, he was fully recovered from the "ideas and humbug recently in vogue" (those of the Revolution).

Kleist referred once again to his illness, which was now over, a lingering weakness would be removed by the baths; but Köckeritz pulled out his handkerchief, blew his nose and admitted his reservations with regard to a man who had left the Army, had now also turned his back on civil life, wandered about abroad and for good measure "made vershes!"

Kleist burst into tears, but refused to give in and made it clear to the General that the projected embarcation in Boulogne should more fittingly come before a medical than a political tribunal, and convinced him to such an extent that Köckeritz began to apologise. He certainly could not give him any hope of the king's favour he sought, but suddenly an opportunity presented itself. Major von Gualtieri, the brother of Kleist's cousin by marriage, his friend Marie von Kleist, was going to Madrid in the summer of 1804 as Prussian Ambassador. If Kleist went as his attaché there might be an opportunity to get into the Diplomatic Service. But Gualtieri's mission was delayed and when Kleist took up relations with his family again and they promised to pay him a small income in Frankfurt, he abandoned his diplomatic prospects. Meanwhile the King had also yielded and Kleist first received a modest appointment in the Ministry in Berlin, then worked on a daily basis in the Crown Land Office in Königsberg. At his family's insistence he was also to carry his fiscal studies to their conclusion.

On 13 May 1805 he announced his arrival in Königsberg to the Prussian Finance Minister Karl von Stein zum Altenstein and told him that he had begun his fiscal and legal studies; he also hoped to be able to take up chemistry again. But aversion for his office seized him almost at once. We learn that he became ill of constipation and headaches. He read a lot, Thomson and Young, above all the *Iliad*. (Kleist is said to have learned Greek in Paris and to have been able to read Homer in the original.) Whether in Königsberg he had become aware, in the circle of officials and officers surrounding von Schön, of the ideas and concepts of national revival is doubtful in view of his completely different interests and poor physical condition.

Napoleon was at the peak of his success. He had set aside the French Republic by becoming Emperor, owned the whole of Italy, half Spain and Germany. The powers had allied themselves against him for the third War of the Coalition in vain. The Prussian patriots wanted to prevent his attack on Austria and were feverish with impatience because the war was being spent in winter quarters while the French overran Austria and encountered heroic resistance in Spain. Kleist wrote in an embittered letter to Rühle von Lilienstern, who was with the army, but on an uneventful front, that the German Empire was about to crumble. He called Napoleon a fortunate adventurer: "Why is there not just one person to send a bullet through the head of this evil spirit of the world? I should like to know what an emigrant like that is doing —"

In another letter Minister Altenstein is urged to influence the king not to allow the cession of Franconia to Napoleon, but in this letter Kleist's professional interests played a part, because he hoped that when he had completed his studies Altenstein

Castle pool in Königsberg (lithograph, mid-19th century)

would give him a post in the Franconian administration. The province had to be reorganized and Kleist joined in the plans for internal reform, which aimed at the removal of the rights of the corporations and the introduction of freedom for the arts and crafts. It is all the more astonishing that in the summer he was already asking the Minister to excuse him. He said his health was so shattered that he must take the waters. He was given leave and went for a few weeks to Pillau, but could only enter the baths two or three times. His nervous system seemed to be in as distressed a state as his digestion. In those tormented months, shut away from the world, Kleist wrote the great tales *Die Marquise von O* and *Michael Kohlhaas,* finished *The Broken Jug,* prepared *Amphitryon* for publication, worked on *Penthesilea* and gave *Earthquake in Chile* its final form. As always, his sickness of body was a crisis of the spirit; the more he arrived, by work, on the track of the enigma of his existence, the more it eased. Now too he found the courage to meet Wilhelmine von Zenge again; she was now the wife of Professor Krug, whom he had up to then been avoiding in Königsberg. He accepted Krug's invitation and read out parts of the Tales from manuscript to a small company in the Krugs' home.

We do not know what was going on inside him at the time. The listeners heard him with friendly expectation; at that time literature in Germany was still regarded as a source of social culture, the poet could still move from the small public of the salon to the big one of the world and vice versa: success in the social circle brought success with a wider public in its train. But what must the aristocratic officers, high officials and professors with their ladies have thought, when Kleist read from *Kohlhaas,* where the Junker plays a disagreeable role, a horsedealer is the hero and men of the Church and princes are unable to control the devil? The *Marquise von O* could not be read aloud at all, since the puzzle-play with the pregnant woman in a swoon was a slap in the face to all morality.

When Prussia was defeated and the last battle at Preussisch-Eylau was lost, Kleist went to Berlin in a state of deep depres-

Prof. Wilhelm Traugott Krug, Luise von Zenge and Krug's wife Wilhelmine née v. Zenge. Silverpoint drawing by Friedrich August Jung (1781—1841)

sion and was imprisoned by the French on entering the city, because he could only present a military discharge but not a civilian pass. He was suspected of being a Schill officer and protests availed him nothing. In February 1807 he was sent with two guards to France under humiliating circumstances, as a criminal. He was first held in Fort des Joux, then in Châlons-sur-Marne. No one could tell him why he had been arrested. People hinted at orders from above. Protests were registered, but without result. Kleist's guards, elderly men, contracted serious diseases. Since the prison administration did not know whether Kleist was supposed to be a Military or civilian prisoner, he did not even receive his pay. For his small expenses he was dependent on contributions from the faithful Ulrike. At last he obtained pen and paper and was allowed to walk on the walls. Not until July did an order come from the French general in Berlin to release him, but by now he lacked the means to return and once again Kleist had to wait for weeks for the money.

The letters of these months sound quite different from those from Königsberg. Kleist suffered his fate with composure, his physical indisposition seemed to have been blown away, the enforced isolation in the fortress was used for writing. More sections of *Penthesilea* came to life here. The isolation in which Kleist wrote this greatest drama of the self-destruction of a human being is symbolic of his relationship to society.

The Mystery of the Lovers

(Amphitryon)

We do not know when Kleist was first inspired by the great concept which converted Molière's theme of the divine paramour of the Theban commander's wife into a poem of mysterious depth. Nothing is so astonishing as the distance between Kleist's life and his work. Whereas much of Goethe's work can be explained by his life, there are no such easy classifications in Kleist. His work is always enormously much more than the life of Kleist the youth and man. In *Amphitryon,* the prototypes of the new man as Kleist saw him are united for the first time. The line runs from Agnes via Eve to Alkmene. Judge Adam is exalted into Jupiter. The grotesque detail, the Sosias action, is separated from the main action in such a way that it runs parallel to it like a satire. Penthesilea, eating the body of her beloved, comprehends the reality of the soul. Jupiter, intent on the enjoyment of the beautiful woman, must understand the connection as a mystery, marriage — in Christian terms — as a sacrament.

The plan to translate Molière's comedy was made on the Swiss journey of 1802. Kleist's friend Zschokke was then working on the translation of Molière's plays into German. The translation appeared in full in 1806, but for *Amphitryon.* It is assumed that Kleist had promised Zschokke that he would do the translation, but his alterations and additions were too significant, the sense of the French comedy of the adulterous god shifted; a drama of his own came into being, and all it had in common with Molière in the end was a sequence of scenes. The subject and characters belonged to Kleist and the decisive fourth scene in Act II does not occur in Molière at all.

Alkmene, wife of the Theban commander Amphitryon, is visited by Jupiter in the form of her husband. Molière develops this into a gallant comedy. The ancient legend produced many forms of the chief of gods, which he assumed in order to make love to the daughters of man. The god was entitled to do this, and the dénouement of the stories, part farcical, part bawdy, always consisted in the exposure of the god as god. This made all tragedy impossible, but not that comedy which touches on the lecherous. From it come the Amphitryon plays of literature.

To someone of Kleist's inclinations and enhanced sensitivity in matters of Eros and sex, the Frenchman's gallant solution could only be a painful one. When, in 1805/6, he was busy with his manuscripts in Königsberg, this material gave him the opportunity to present his own problem: here all the stones of the arch were assembled — that arch which is maintained by the fact that every stone is doing its best to fall.

The characters of the play form parallel triangles: Jupiter-Alkmene-Amphitryon and Mercury-Charys-Sosias. The poles are heaven and earth, Kleist's heaven and Kleist's earth. The theme of divine love is given its variations on the terrestrial level: Sosias has no feeling for Alkmene's sufferings. What in her is certainty, moved by 'feeling', has to be thrashed into him with a stick. In these grotesque scenes, scorning and parodying antiquity and its myths, Kleist discovered an antiquity which was far from emotional, far from enlightened. Sosias and Charys, with Mercury, belong to the family of the Aristophanes type of non-heroes, just as Alkmene is a daughter of the most tragic of the tragic dramatists, Euripides. At the same time Alkmene is more than a character of antiquity. Her conduct towards husband and gods is unthinkable without the Christian religion, with its harmonization and unification with God and its sanctification of married love, since the lovers can only be united in God. For the first time Kleist has here shown how the *miracle of love* — otherwise set down as a naked fact — is conceivable and understandable. The loneliness of the ego is shattered in the mystery of love.

Jupiter, all Greek God, pursues Alkmene ever deeper into confusion and is jubilant at the sweetness of that confusion. The earthly form has to give way to the divine image, even *Käthchen* dreams of her lover before she possesses him, just as the *Prince of Homburg* dreams of the fame he has yet to win. But in Kleist the terrestrial is a sign pointing to the exalted. He felt the tension more clearly and more "idealistically" than Schiller, whose characters tend towards an abstract ideal. In Goethe's *Faust* the opposing worlds are obvious; everyone can discover the two souls within him as a sensual and a spiritual one. In Kleist the problem assumes an unavoidable, pressing nature, where delight and torment are mingled, just as modern man experiences. Alkmene suffers incomparably more purely and profoundly than the heroes and heroines of the classical-romantic age in which Kleist's life was lived. Kleist's *Amphitryon* does not live because of an extreme, but because of a deeper-lying image, in which the play of all the poles is visible simultaneously. What is farce on the one hand becomes mystery on the other. Kleist's language bears witness to both at once. The gaze is constantly directed from the banal to the most exalted, constantly making sure that above the enigmatic, disturbed and fragile world an absolute order exists, as its form and law. No earthly spouse can correspond to the divine idol and so it transpires that the most innocent of the innocent, Alkmene, like the *Marquise von O,* sends her true husband away. Overwhelming deception, blessed delusion! Then is not injustice done to the commander-in-chief? Yes and no, for the dialectic is resolved when the eagle of the god hovers over the

Scene from Kleist's "Amphitryon"
(E. W. Borchert, Liselotte Schreiner, Werner Hinz)

scene. Jupiter, ultimately all-powerful, promises the highest to the man, Amphitryon, in "his" son, Alkmene's child, Hercules.

Alkmene, unconscious, utters an "Ah" in reply. She is all sweetness, as obedient as she is intelligent, and accepts what will remain for her an indistinguishable blending of appearance and idealized image. The linguistic stylization takes its source from the biblical Annunciation; that "Ah" of Alkmene enshrines a "Be it unto me according to Thy Word".

What the world makes of it is as clear in Jupiter as it is in Alkmene, who is tortured, and Amphitryon who is horned. All the puzzles are parallel and intertwined. Jupiter needs man as man needs god, the absolute is also a stone in the arch and meaningless in isolation. This should not be seen as relativism. Kleist's theological creed was that man was created in the image of God and God decreed the ascension of men to paradise for His glory. For Kleist, heaven was not above earth, nor the idea above reality; paradise appeared as a bright point on an infinite line where the ego says yes to itself and reality serves it. The story of *The Duel* tells of the defence of innocence, although the lady's innocence is very improbable, and even divine justice — in which one believes and must believe as the ultimate authority — apparently decides against her, and here comes the tenet that angels guard the head of innocence.

Penthesilea and Käthchen

Kleist, the Prussian refugee, went to Dresden, where old friends such as Rühle and Pfuel and new ones such as Adam Müller and Ludwig Tieck were living. The Schlieben and Körner families were there. The elder Körner had charge of the *Amphitryon* and was looking for a publisher for it. Kleist was a friendly visitor to the von Haza family, to one or two professors and in particular to the Austrian Chargé d'Affaires, Count von Buol-Mühlingen, a henchman of Count Stadion in Vienna. Since Prussia had given up the struggle against the tyrant, Stadions' Austria was the hope of the patriots. In Buol's house *Amphitryon* was read aloud and newspaper articles appeared in Dresden for the first time referring to the "presence of one of the most outstanding living writers, Herr von Kleist". In Buol's house an amateur performance of *The Broken Jug* was arranged. Buol tried to recommend Kleist to Count Ferdinand Pálffy, Director of the Vienna Burgtheater. For the first time the poet found a select public for his plays and novellas. Buol's house and Adam Müller's skill as a publicist gave Kleist the greatest reputation he ever achieved. One evening he received a symbolic laurel wreath here at a public dinner.

Since his second Swiss journey, Kleist had always had a manuscript of *Penthesilea* with him. There is ample witness to the anecdote which tells of Kleist exploding into Pfuel's room one evening with every sign of distraction, crying: "She is dead, oh, she is dead!" and when the company sprang up in horror, asking *who* was dead: "Penthesilea, my Penthesilea is dead!" The main work on the play was probably done in Königsberg and Châlons. Now, in Dresden in the summer of 1807, it was finished. In June 1808 Kleist offered it to Cotta for publication.

Penthesilea and Käthchen belong together, they stem from the same line of the enraptured who know not what they do and cannot explain deeds which remain incomprehensible to reason. Penthesilea's horror when she is told that she tore her beloved Achilles' body with her teeth in company with her hounds, corresponds to Käthchen's reverie in the scene under the elder-bush. Kleist wrote in December 1808 to Heinrich Josef von Collin, the Austrian writer who had helped smooth the way to the Burgtheater: "Anyone who loves Käthchen cannot lack all understanding for Penthesilea; they go together like the + and − of algebra and are one and the same being, but conceived under opposite conditions."

The play takes place in 24 scenes without acts, on the battlefield of Troy. Under the leadership of their queen Penthesilea the Amazon army advances from Asia Minor. The Trojans hope to be relieved by them and experience their first disappointment when the women fling themselves on the corps sent to welcome them. The Greeks, with the deludedness of gloriously obtuse heroes, for their part regard the Amazons as allies, but are dismissed with similar savagery.

Penthesilea and Achilles meet on the battlefield; she is seeking the son of Thetis and he is seeking her. This meeting, which is love, takes place under the star of battle. The Amazons, manless as they are, must find a man in the battle whom they will lead off to the Rose Festival of ineffable union. The invention of the myth is largely Kleist's own work. He knew only from hearsay the legend of the Amazons in which Achilles kills Penthesilea — or vice versa. The legend of the founding of the Amazon state and the association of its foundation with the fate of the heroine were invented by him. This alone is evidence of Kleist's mastery of material and characters.

Achilles, in the great line of lovers, was unaware of the Amazon law. He voluntarily allows himself to be captured, to win Penthesilea in the sweet captivity of the Rose Festival. When she discovers that she has not conquered her hero but he has seduced her, she turns into a fury. For the first time, Kleist's annihilatory rage appears, personified in her in association with Eros. Kisses and bites rhyme, says Penthesilea. Love and death become one in intoxication, death is fulfilment, the world of the battlefield.

Dammed, divided, dismembered, hacked to pieces, then gathered together and released like lightning, Kleist's literary language became the expression for the "soul-destroying course of events". Penthesilea is unique and her uniqueness conceals tragedy within it. She cannot escape the imperative of her actuality, consisting of the desire to dominate, attachment to the State and its mores, unnatural law, masochism, maidenly modesty and erotic obsession, because she is Penthesilea. She is by no means "man", or Kleistian man, she is neither image nor pattern. What exists, exists according to categories whos principles lie in the ego; all metaphysics had become "mythology" for Kleist — and now his self-constructed world is carried to absurdity. What others say is not believed; Penthesilea will not believe that she has destroyed Achilles: "And if it were written with lightning in the night and if the voice of the thunder told me it, I would still cry to both: You lie". Kleist was creating a

Achilles killing Penthesilea (Greek bowl, Munich)

new human being here and immediately overthrowing her. Penthesilea dies as she realizes that the premises of this new world and her existence do not coincide.

It is difficult to perform Kleist's *Penthesilea* on stage. This is not only because of the complicated psychology and mythical costume, it is due above all to the poetic diction, full of metaphor, for which there is scarcely any parallel in German literature. Since Kleist's real models were the plays of Greek antiquity, when the gods were believed in and gods and heroes trod the stage as leading characters, the truth of his plays lies in an element which has become alien to the modern theatre. The difficulty with *Käthchen von Heilbronn* is similar; it is a medieval drama of chivalry. But the characters in both plays are "modern". A performance (and translation into modern languages) must therefore be simultaneously ancient (or medieval) and modern. This was possible in the genius of Kleist's language; performances can never do more than approach the poetic truth of a Kleist play.

Kleist was aware of the matter. He sent *Penthesilea* to Goethe on 24 January 1808, with a famous letter in which he says that he is presenting himself "on the knees of my heart". He emphasizes that this play is no more written for the stage than his earlier one, *The Broken Jug,* which Goethe had put on in Weimar. Goethe felt disagreeably moved and replied: "Permit me to say that it always troubles and distresses me when I see young men of spirit and talent waiting for a theatre which is to come. A Jew waiting for the Messiah, a Christ for the New Jerusalem or a Portuguese for Don Sebastian do not give me greater discomfort. Before every trestle-work of boards I want to say to the true theatrical genius: 'Hic Rhodus, hic salta!' At every fair I undertake, on planks balanced on barrels, to give the greatest pleasure to the cultivated and uncultivated masses, mutatis mutandis, with Calderòn's plays."

Goethe was both right and wrong. Instinctively he rejected Kleist for his daemonic qualities, his wildness. Kleist had touched on things with which Goethe did not wish to be associated since transferring to Weimar: he knew that they threatened him. Just as Lessing had once rejected Goethe, as Schiller turned Hölderlin away, so Goethe thrust the greatest dramatist of the age away from him. In a clear-sighted epigram Kleist retorted to the Olympian of Weimar that "in age he dissolved the beam his youth once shed."

Käthchen von Heilbronn is subtitled "Ordeal by Fire, a great historical drama of chivalry". Never again was Kleist to absorb so much of what is popularly called romanticism, medieval scenery, knights and maidens in castles, honest citizens with beautiful daughters, the Holy Vehmic Court, trial by ordeal and the Imperial might transcending all earthly justice. Like the scenery, the action of the play draws its life from

Scene from "Penthesilea" (Maria Wimmer, Heinz Baumann)

fairy-tale and legendary features, from naïve piety and bottomless falsehood.

Where Alkmene was a princess, Penthesilea a heroine, Käthchen was a child of the people, her rank the same, and only the more gracious because her social position makes it moving. She follows Count von Strahl step by step, until Theobald accuses him of sorcery, for no girl had ever followed her beloved with such dog-like, blind devotion. She had flung herself to the street from a window thirty feet high and followed him although her pelvis was broken: the victory of mind over matter. The subject characterizes contempt for what was Penthesilea's pride, the body. Similar scenes are repeated, for instance Käthchen is sent by her wicked rival Kunigunde into a burning castle; it collapses on her but a cherub, which becomes visible, protects her. Her love for the Count is an unending dream; she says constantly: "Yes, my great lord," or "Don't know, my great lord." Like all Kleist's heroes she swoons when the forces of the heart are overstretched, in this case, when the Count orders her to return to her father.

The second act begins in a cave in the forest. The Count becomes aware of his love for Käthchen in exuberant language, making use of oriental images, unknown elsewhere in good literature.

The world is a paradise of love transposed into a dream, sensually glowing, headily enraptured — but the progress of the action breaks off, the scene alters drastically to another environment and other figures. It is as if a farce began now, as the Rhineland Count announces a feud against Kunigunde for three towns and seventeen villages, calling her a "raging virago" who has already sent three knights of the Empire down on him over the same matter. Kunigunde is to be kidnapped and imprisoned in a charcoal-burner's hut, there is a fierce storm outside, but Count Friedrich frees her, chance playing a major role, and leads the surprised captive bride to his mother's castle. "As truly as I am a man, I desire you to wife." What has become of Käthchen?

78

Scene from "Käthchen von Heilbronn" (Elisabeth Lennartz, Carl Ebert)

The Count has dreamed on Christmas Eve that he will marry a daughter of the Emperor. Since Kunigunde is descended from the Saxon Emperors he thinks he is fulfilling the dream. Kunigunde, made young and beautiful, with the help of her dressing table, is in reality an ugly bag of bones, but the world of men can be deceived all too easily. The Count slowly recognizes that Kunigunde is a false Emperor's daughter, Käthchen the right one. Roughly from the fourth act onwards, the play loses its tragic undertones since a good outcome is in prospect: Käthchen's white magic will conquer Kunigunde's black, and that Christmas Eve ends in fulfilment after all, for Käthchen, who had dreamed of the Count as her husband on the same night as he was dreaming of her, *is* an Emperor's daughter; his Majesty remembers seducing a citizen's daughter sixteen years before, in Heilbronn.

This leaves the play open to reproach; the finest of the fine, the Heilbronn armourer, has been cuckolded, and it is a part of the naïve, fairytale attributes of the play that through his explanation, Imperial Majesty may and can restore the injured honour of a man, even in the most intimate matters. Nevertheless, there is something left out, and Kleist, who left no theme unresolved, took this subject to its conclusion in *Amphitryon,* where the adulterer is a god.

Phoebus

When, a few years later, Brentano met Kleist in Berlin, he spoke of Kleist's *Phoebus* with an ironic accent. The establishment and editorship of *Phoebus* were closely connected with Kleist's renewed appearance on the literary scene. On the advice of Judge Christian Gottfried Körner, father of the writer, who had already been helpful to Schiller, Kleist had decided to open a publisher's and bookseller's business in Dresden. To this end he borrowed money from his friends Rühle and Pfuel. But since they were not much richer than the bookseller-to-be, Kleist asked Ulrike for a subsidy and even tried to persuade her to invest her modest fortune in the undertaking, apart from the urgently needed 500 Thaler, promising her interest of 22%. Fortunately Ulrike knew better.

There were five booksellers in Dresden at the time. Understandably, they took a jaundiced view of this enterprise of Kleist the outsider. Kleist's real partner on the editorial board and in the business was to be Adam Müller, who enjoyed great social and business esteem and held courses for the diplomats accredited to Dresden on the connection between mind and politics, economy and people. His famous work *Die Lehre vom Gegensatze* (The Doctrine of Antithesis) had appeared in 1804. By "antithesis" Müller meant the poles of positive and negative, subject and object, science and religion, nature and art. In contrast to the absolutist philosophy, he wanted to overcome the dualistic confrontations of the Enlightenment and postulated an organic view of the world, symbolized by the sphere, an "ever-fitting metaphor" from astronomy, where balance prevails through the interaction of attraction and repulsion.

According to Müller, reality consists only in "concrete situation" and is in every case the result of oppositions, that is subjective and objective conditions, as we would say: both-and, ambivalence, egocentricity and otherdirectedness. Müller explains the revolutionary state of the politico-social world by the abstract mode of thought and feeling, the rigid pattern of the adherents of the Enlightenment and their ideological limitations. Here his model is Edmund Burke, the English opponent of Jacobinism. In the sciences, the writings of Goethe, I. W. Ritter, Steffen and Schelling are important to him because they show that nature and life are organic states, units of development. Accordingly, for him the people means more than the population of a strip of land, more than the subject and object of economic processes; it is in fact an evolved community with

81

immanent laws. Müller's philosophy is directed more towards Fichte than Kant.

Kleist felt drawn to Müller, the great speaker and pedagogue, for like Kleist, Müller had a foretaste of the future in his blood (philosophically he is Hegel's predecessor) and preferred the balancing out of a number of possibilities to linear ideologies. As a human being he was distinguished, even elegant, attractive to women, and exerted an influence on Kleist because he brought the chaos lived by Kleist if not into a system, at least into a method. Socially and literarily he encouraged Kleist to the utmost, bore with his changing moods and temper with the greatest patience and although they often quarrelled, they always made it up.

This Müller is supposed to have arranged for a publication whose acquisition at that time would have been sufficient to carry the proposed publishing house through all possible dangers: the German edition of the *Code Napoléon*. It did seem that the whole of Germany was going to become French at that

Adam Müller (1779—1829) who produced "Phöbus" with Kleist

82

time[1]. The introduction of the uniform Code into the German language area, with its fragmented administration, promised to be a huge commercial success. On 25 October 1807 Kleist wrote to Ulrike:

"It is not impossible that we shall be publishing the Codex Napoleon and that our house will in general be selected by the French Government to disseminate their publications in Germany; as you can easily imagine, this would mean that the whole basis of the institute would be established at a stroke. You will not be over-hasty in drawing political conclusions from this step . . ."

But the affair miscarried and for this reason the idea of book publishing had to be abandoned. The only other project was an edition of the works of Novalis, made available by the Hardenberg family, but this also miscarried because the family wanted a luxury edition and there was not enough money available for this. This is the explanation of the appearance of parts of Novalis' hitherto unpublished works in *Phoebus.* When the journal was being planned Kleist was prepared to bestow a character on it with his own works. He wrote to the big German publishing companies discreetly, asking them to commission his journal, which was to be brought out by the editors themselves. Here lay a failure in calculation, for it was to turn out that the publishing trade was not inclined to procure business for the outsiders.

Initially everything looked favourable. Subscription lists were circulated in society and there were fifty subscribers in Dresden alone. Kleist appealed to Goethe, Wieland, Jean Paul and Collin for contributions, made much of the unpublished Novalis works and Adam Müller's editorship, wrote to his former superiors in Königsberg: Auerswald, von Schön and

---

[1] In many German theatres plays were still acted only in French. This is one of the external reasons why Kleist found so few theatres to perform his plays.

Altenstein. He had hopes of acquiring the public interested in Schiller's *Horae,* but gravely overestimated their number at 3,000. The journal was to be illustrated with large plates, etchings by Ferdinand Hartmann, for as the title states, it was to be a journal for the Arts, elegantly produced in quarto. By "Arts" the editors meant literature, the graphic arts, theatre and foreign literature. They intended to be completely neutral as to politics.

The first number of the journal appeared at the end of January 1808, adorned with an etching showing the young Phoebus in the sun-chariot with four steeds, above the silhouette of a town with bridges and towers. The town was unmistakably Dresden. Even the delay in the first issue was a poor sign. The resident book trade were set against the enterprise, but Kleist considered: "In view of our literary and political connections, we cannot fail to get the whole trade to ourselves."

Today *Phoebus* is one of the great treasures of the bibliophile market, not least because of the first impressions it contains. There is an *Organic fragment from the tragedy: Penthesilea,* covering 27 pages. Also published here were Kleist's verse legends *Der Engel am Grabe des Herrn* (The Angel at the Lord's Graveside), *Die Marquise von O* (The Marchioness of O), extracts from *The Broken Jug,* the fragment *Robert Guiskard, Michael Kohlhaas* and extracts from *Käthchen von Heilbronn.* The issues also contained the first publication of pieces by Novalis (e. g. the poem "Soll dieser Blick voll Huld und Süsse . . ." (Shall this glance filled with grace and sweetness . . . under the title 'To Dorothee'), Adam Müller, Adam Oehlenschläger and F. G. Wetzel. The sixth issue contained Schiller's "La fête de la victoire ou la retour des grecques", translated by Madame de Staël-Holstein, in French. Hopes of contributions from Goethe, Wieland and Jean Paul were not fulfilled. The last issue of Phoebus appeared at the end of 1808.

At the turn of the year 1808/9 events had arisen which were to divert Kleist from the literary and artistic ambitions of

Phöbus.

Ein Journal für die Kunst.

Herausgegeben

von

Heinrich v. Kleist und *Adam H. Müller.*

Erster Jahrgang.

Mit Kupfern.

Eilftes u. Zwölftes Stück. Novbr. u. Decbr. 1808.

Dresden,
im Verlage der Waltherschen Hofbuchhandlung.

Phoebus. The hopes he had placed in it were no more fulfilled than those he had placed in Müller. In Austria the struggle for freedom against Napoleon had broken out. Kleist's contribution to it was a new play, *Die Hermannschlacht* (The Warrior's Battle) and he hoped for a performance in Vienna. The play appealed to political and strategic hopes; its mood was decisively intensified at the moment of revolt under the pressure of the political situation. Only now did Kleist give full rein to his anti-French inclinations. He believed that, as with the Spanish revolt, a turn of events was about to take place in Austria. Its abrupt failure was one of the causes of Kleist's nervous exaltation which led to his death.

The Freedom of the Nation
(The Warrior's Battle, a Political Poem)

On 1 January 1809 Kleist offered his play *Die Hermanns-schlacht* (The Warrior's Battle) to the Vienna Burgtheater through Collin. He wanted it to appear on the stage in advance of *Käthchen von Heilbronn,* for he thought that the great moment of Germany's liberation from Rome (from Napoleon) was at hand. In December the French troops had largely evacuated Prussia, because their Emperor needed them for the conquest of Spain. In mid-December 1808 Major Schill had made a tumultuously applauded entry into Berlin, the king and even Freiherr vom Stein had returned to the capital, although Stein soon had to flee to Russia after having been proscribed by Napoleon.

But Kleist was not waiting for Prussia but for Austria, which had modernized and expanded its army, whereas the princes of the Rhine Alliance, Bavaria, and Saxony were ranged with Napoleon and Prussia was slowly beginning to set up a small army. Austria hoped to carry the North Germans with it by an

Archduke Charles of Austria at the Battle of Aspern

initial success against Napoleon. Kleist wanted to go to Vienna with the Imperial Embassy if it had to leave Dresden. But only on 29 April, when Buol had already left Dresden, did he succeed, leaving debts behind him, in leaving Dresden for Austria. His travelling companion was Friedrich Christoph Dahlmann, the subsequent historian. They reached Vienna just after the battle of Aspern and visited the battlefield where there were still some wounded. Archduke Karl's victory over Napoleon seemed to confirm the patriots' expectations, having shown that Napoleon could be defeated. The North Germans were not exactly rapturously greeted by the Austrians, for Kleist read out some of his own patriotic poems to the dazed soldiers to prove his allegiance. Mistrust of these gentlemen with their high German speech increased when Kleist introduced himself. He was within an ace of being arrested as a relative of the general who had handed over Magdeburg to the French. An obliging officer led them to Headquarters, where the identity of the travellers was confirmed.

F. C. Dahlmann (1785—1860)

The military reversal at Wagram seemed for the moment to have destroyed all hopes of liberation. Instead of staying in Vienna, Dahlmann and Kleist went to Prague, since Bohemia was the only central European country still safe from the French. Since the occupation of Vienna there could be no further thought of a performance of the *Hermannsschlacht* and in view of the bias of the play, which was obvious to any contemporary reader, publication was equally impossible.

In *Amphitryon*, Alcmene's question as to the identity of her husband had quite unexpectedly been solved by Jupiter. Asking and seeking in an empty, as it were abstract space, is cut off by the revelation of the god, this is the answer which contains all causes within itself. Morality is unimportant where a higher law replaces the lower. Transferred into the political sphere this means that the right of the people is higher than that of the legitimate monarch, the right of the natural community transcends that of the individual. In a contribution written for *Germania,* planned in Prague, "On the Salvation of Austria", it said: "First of all, the government of Austria must persuade itself that the war it is waging will be waged neither for glory nor for independence nor even for the existence of her throne, which as things stand, are merely mean and inferior purposes, but for God, Freedom, Law and Morality, for the improvement of a sunken and degenerate generation, in short for goods above all estimation, which must be defended at any price, no matter what, against the enemy assailing them."

Kleist's writing and poetry in the name of Germany were not the result of nationalism but of resistance to oppression by Napoleon; not against the French, whose language he spoke and whose literature he esteemed, but against Napoleon "and so long as he is their Emperor, the French". Underlying Kleist's patriotic feeling is the idea of freedom and justice. The tenets developed by him in the *Cathechism of the Germans,* composed on the pattern of the Spanish revolt, are more connected with the moral than with the political idea of the Kingdom of the Germans. It is the question as to the "concrete situation" which finds an answer in these articles in the Emperor Franz and the Kingdom of the Germans. The Germans are by no means an ideal people. Even the "patricidal ghost" of Napoleon, "risen from hell" ... "who steals about in the Temple of Nature, rattling all the pillars on which it is built", possesses many virtues, cunning, skill, boldness and genius in the field, and is therefore worthy of admiration and honour. "But to admire him now would be just as ruinous as if, at the moment when he threw me in the mud and kicked my face in, I were to admire a wrestler for his strength." Napoleon can be admired only when he has been destroyed.

Kleist's patriotism was nourished on this kind of dialectic; it would never have arisen, had Napoleon not aroused the demon. Kleist did not see the causes of defeat in the greatness of Napoleon and the military and moral superiority of the French. He draws a sharp and stern picture of the causes of the German downfall, and finds two reasons for it. He accuses the Germans of having theorized, thought, pondered too much, where decisive action would have been called for. By this he means the German inclination to overcome problems by reason, through the speculative philosophy of Kant and Fichte on the one hand and on the other hand through the superficial empiricism of the citizenry, with their moral arguments. Owing to this, *true feeling*, the *old mysterious power of the heart,* had fallen short. The Spanish freedom fighters had not wondered and speculated for long as to whether and how they could remove French military domination, but, following their natural patriotic emotions, had taken up arms. What Kleist blamed in Prussia was the hesitation, the political, commercial and intellectual collaboration with the enemy.

Kleist lists the reasons why it had to be so: the desire for wellbeing and enjoyment which had arisen in the last decades, with the rise of the bourgeoisie. To the question as to what the Germans might love with an unbridled and dishonourable love, his Catechism replies: Gold and goods; they traded and trafficked until the sweat dripped from their brows, positively

Hermann's grave. Painting by Caspar David Friedrich

enough to arouse compassion; they thought that a peacefully comfortable and carefree life was all that could be achieved in the world. Yet the highest goods of the world are *God, Fatherland, Emperor* (the German emperor in Vienna — not the Prussian king in Berlin), *Freedom, Love and Faith, Beauty, Knowledge and Art.* These are the ideals for which Hermann fights against Rome.

Up to now, history has been a mythical backcloth for Kleist; in *Penthesilea* he had used the Amazon myth, in *Käthchen von Heilbronn* the medieval Empire. In *Hermannsschlacht* history has become a transparent costume. Varus is Napoleon, Hermann a German Patriot. Marbod represents hesitant southern Germany and must be won over by success. Varus' allies, the Germanic princes Fust, Gueltar and Aristan, are the states of the Rhineland Federation allied to Napoleon, Saxony and Bavaria. Hermann's role seems obscure and ambiguous to the other princes. They interpret his hesitation as cowardice and cannot understand that this hesitation is a tactical trick; Hermann actually knows how numerous and powerful the enemy who has brought half the world under his heel is. He cannot be met with a political coalition alone; a climate of committed resistance, hatred and injury must be created. The dramatic action corresponds to this purpose.

Hermann, prince of the Cherusci and recognized leader of the peoples of northern Germania, will acknowledge the supreme command of all Germany desired by Marbod, leader of the southern tribes, if Marbod will join in Hermann's plan of war to destroy the Romans. Ventidius, the Roman envoy to Hermann, is playing a double game, as Varus is; Rome is trying to play off the German tribes against each other by concluding treaties of friendship with individual peoples. The Romans are so certain of the Germanic discord that an amalgamation of Marbod and Hermann is inconceivable to them. Political dialectic sees "treason" here and the dialectic of the political cat-and-mouse game produces the dramatic character of the play.

The outcome is the celebration of the union of the oppressed against the oppressors, not of one nation against another. Varus and Ventidius are caught in the snares they laid for the Germans. When at the end Hermann and Marbod defeat the Roman army in the Teutoburg Forest, the claim to freedom is victorious over tyranny. There are some situations in the *Hermannsschlacht* which give unpleasant pause to one's interpretation: the feigned fondness of Thusnelda for Ventidius and his end in the bear-pit, or the coldly calculating way in which Hermann waits until success is inevitable. Hermann's own willingness for sacrifice demands the same of everyone else.

The connection between the *Hermannsschlacht* and Kleist's view of the world cannot be grasped through the medium of the suffering subject. Here for the first time the suffering and acting ego comes out of itself and is brought into service. After ten years, Kleist had found the way to community. This is the

Paul Hartmann as Hermann in Kleist's "Hermannsschlacht"

entirely personal meaning of his turning to the fatherland. Here the fatherland is Germany, whereas in the *Prince of Homburg* it was to be called Prussia. Not that Kleist had withdrawn in the space of a year from a German to a Prussian fatherland: both countries are symbols within the totality of the poetic subject of a greater one, of a common existence where man is no longer confronted with chaos. Germany, or Prussia, are literary places, where human freedom has a meaning. They are not absolute values but nominal symbols where people could live with as much freedom and dignity as Goethe's *Iphigenie in Tauris* or the heroes of the classical French theatre in Rome or Athens.

On the other hand it would be a misunderstanding of Kleist's essence to regard the oaths and imprecations of his summonses and challenges as Romantic poetry, which were not also directed at the object of their utterances. The political situation had made hatred for Napoleon and his Frenchmen into something very concrete. It was the fortune of the day that Kleist found in Napoleon an object of world stature for his hatred: without the Napoleonic hegemony Kleist's hatred would not have become so daemonic. With his Prussian background, Kleist had trodden the traditions of his family underfoot. He had left the Service, was regarded with suspicion by King and Court, had alienated the family and withdrawn from his friends. Here, in Dresden, it all broke through in an almost pathological way. Like the rage of Penthesilea, people were astounded at Hermann's hatred of Rome. Where was Kleist's spiritual home? His age could not understand him, because it did not understand his dreams of paradise, this indescribable mingling of reality and dreams. The *Hermannsschlacht* was not printed until Wilhelm Tieck took it on in 1821 and then it was misinterpreted for another century.

If the events of 1809 far transcended the immediate hour of the *Hermannsschlacht*, from Prague Kleist tried to exert an influence by founding a new journal, the *Germania.* He wrote to Friedrich Schlegel in Vienna:

"Very dear Herr von Schlegel,

Obristburggraf (Colonel-Burggrave), Count von Wallis has submitted to His Excellency Count von Stadion an application which Herr von Dahlmann and I had handed in to the Government, asking permission to publish a journal, or in reality a weekly paper, under the title of *Germania*. You can easily imagine what this paper is to contain; there is only one subject of discussion for a German now. Herr von Dahlmann and I agreed to ask you to use your good offices with the Count to do what ever may be necessary in order to obtain the permission under discussion, and that as quickly as circumstances allow. To this appeal we add yet another, which is almost equally important to us: namely to be kind enough to present us with contributions, or at least with *one* for the time being, until the offers of the bookdealers enable us to recompense you like anyone else. It goes without saying that (if the remittance is not

Prague at the beginning of the 19th century (steel engraving)

95

too much) we would at once adorn one of the first issues with it; less to honour you, of which you have no need, than ourselves and our institute. With its publication I desire nothing more (— for I feel myself capable of directing it personally only for want of a better) than to create for our writers, and particularly the north German ones, an opportunity to put into my pages with impunity what they have to say to the people. We are not naming ourselves; nor any other for that matter, unless it is expressly required. Looking forward to a favourable answer soon, I close with the assurance of my heartfelt respect and love and remain, Herr von Schlegel, your most obedient

Heinrich von Kleist."

The letter was written in Prague on 13 June 1809. The journal did not appear. The great movement of the war collapsed and that meant the end of Kleist's intention to fling himself directly or indirectly into the current of events, as he confessed to Ulrike. Prague had become a refuge, which was not part of his plans. Of course, he met Buol who introduced him to all kinds of people, including Count von Kolowrat, in whose palace promises were made to promote the plan of the weekly paper to publisher and authorities, but the setback at Wagram reduced all their hopes to nought. Kleist fell into one of his severe sicknesses. Once again, his excess of feeling had been disappointed by the *fragility* of the world. He was nursed for long weeks in the monastery of the Brothers of Mercy in Prague, while his friends in Berlin thought him missing or dead. We know virtually nothing about these months of his life.

This year saw not only Kleist's appeals and summonses to politics, the *Katechismus der Deutschen* (Catechism for the Germans) and some satirical letters which had in part been intended as contributions to *Germania,* but also the political poems.

With these poems, which include the *Kriegslied* (War Song) the songs *An Franz den Ersten, Kaiser von Oesterreich* (To Francis I, Emperor of Austria) and *An Palafox* (To Palafox), the

Queen Luise in her family circle (Painting by Dähling, 1807)

Spanish general, *Germania an Ihre Kinder, an den Erzherzog Karl* (Germania to her children, for Archduke Charles) as well as the Ode on the Entry of the King into Berlin in December 1809 and — a little later — the Birthday Poem to Queen Luise which is extant in three versions, Kleist made the most powerful poetic contribution to the wars of freedom. The poems of the rest, Stolberg, Brentano, Arnim, Körner, Arndt, never achieved this form; they are either popular patriotic poems or privately emotional ones; these poets were never able to make their poems written to or about people into the representative expression of the spirit of the age. For one moment of tremendous excitement, Kleist seems to have become the voice of the nation.

Kleist's poems are unique in German literature. Their content and tone are not paralleled by the poems of that time. They come from the depths of his soul, which felt itself to be alone and unhappy and was always trying to perceive a spark of paradise from the depths of humiliation by the world, with its fraudulent and illusory character. This spark was in Kleist's inmost heart and he would have liked to make it into a mighty fire. For however distracted, contradictory and hopeless he often seemed to be, yet the fire was still burning deep within, a silent, chaste and even comely flame, to which his portraits of women bear witness. Not until Kleist analysed the forces of his spirit with reason and his pure intentions were challenged and deranged by the way of the wicked world, did his humility turn into confusion, and he tried to exact what can only be a gift. The musicality of which there is so much evidence went into his poems in both rhythm and tone: they must be read aloud in order to take on the fullness with which they originated.

He believed in his "vocation" and was anxious not to fail it. If he was to be close to the political events of the decisive Austrian area, he also saw in this a "divine mission" which can only be interpreted on religious lines. He was more deeply permeated by a "holy" sense of duty than the Romantics of his period, who often sound a frivolous, affected note, smacking of literary tactics. In the months of the winter of 1808/9 Kleist thought he had come closer to his vocation than ever before, since what was dear to *him* was dear to the whole nation — or should have been dear. For the first time he felt released from the prison of his soul.

Michael Kohlhaas

In the novella *Michael Kohlhaas* Kleist reflected the stages of his relationship to and understanding of the world as nowhere else. They precisely parallel the story of a man who takes the right which society has denied him. The success which Kohlhaas wins from life in his death is of a simplicity which can move to tears. The tale begins with revolt because of a relatively small injustice performed by the Junkers of the Tronkenburg against the horse-dealer Kohlhaas, when they maltreat the black horses he has had to leave behind as enforced security. When Kohlhaas is unable to reach the powerful lords through the law he feels justified in self-help and takes a gang of plunderers and arsonists to despoil the land of the Prince, who, as he must think, has denied him his right.

The Tronkenburg and its Junkers are the symbol of the despicable world of the extortionists, ne'er-do-wells, gluttons, guzzlers and blackguards, who victimise the world with tolls and turnpikes, dogs, abuse of office, delays and obstructionism. Behind them rises the abundantly abstract sphere of "justice" to which Kohlhaas appeals in all good faith in the person of its most distinguished representative, the Elector. But he finds out that the ne'er-do-wells and blackguards have their cousins and brothers-in-law at Court and turn the ideal world of justice into a farce by intrigues, embezzlement, lawyers' tricks and knowledge of processes which are impenetrable to the ordinary mortal. Kohlhaas' first acts of open warfare simply introduce the story, for the horse-dealer accedes to the phoney peace of the amnesty transmitted by Luther and goes to Dresden, where they are amiable towards him at first and the legal business goes in his favour — until bureaucracy gains its ascendancy, almost foreshadowing Franz Kafka, and the net is drawn tight over Kohlhaas' head.

The world's disarray is constantly displayed to us in the story, shattering, threatening, seldom entertaining. It becomes clearest where the authorities of justice, the courts, the judges, the administrative bureaucracy and finally the Saxon prince whose verdict is benevolent and yet who becomes weak in the face of evil, show themselves to be perverted. In breach of the promised amnesty, a grisly verdict is pronounced on the horse-dealer: "To be pinched with red-hot tongs by the flayer's-men, quartered and his body burned between wheel and gallows."

The impressive episode in which Kohlhaas turns to Martin Luther, the ultimate earthly authority for him, and his hope, which does not deceive him, of justice and intercession — this episode sets to rights Kohlhaas' initial temptation to see himself as the representative of the Archangel Michael on earth. He voluntarily submits to Luther's judgement and when Luther ('building on a sound element in the breast of the incendiary') after an initial withdrawal, recognises Kohlhaas' case as just, Kohlhaas for his part asks the holy man for "the comfort of the Divine Sacrament" and Luther agrees, on condition that Kohlhaas forgives his enemy, as it is Christian to do. Kohlhaas:

"'Right Reverend Sir', said Kohlhaas, blushing as he grasped his hand, — 'now?' — 'Even the Lord did not forgive all his enemies . . .'"

The Luther scene was in no way, as one hears claimed, intended by Kleist to be a resolution of the problem in the spirit of religion. In that case it would have been dealt with and, like his wife, Lisbeth, Kohlhaas could have closed his eyes for ever with a word of forgiveness. For Kohlhaas-Kleist, the religious solution of the problem would not be a solution but an escape.

The introduction of Luther and the hero's talk with him have a functional significance in the economy of the epic: they show Kohlhaas having renounced all the fanatically sectarian ideology of his deed and seeking a just settlement from a source which is morally integral, after State, prince, councils and bureaucracy — the proper purveyors of the justice which is sought — have failed. Luther makes an acceptable compromise proposal to the prince, which is in fact accepted, but later appears inverted into its opposite in the thicket of the processes of intrigue, so that this death sentence is pronounced on Kohlhaas.

"Affairs stood thus for the unfortunate Kohlhaas in Dresden when the Elector of Brandenburg intervened to save him from the arbitrary hands of the superior power and reclaimed him as a Brandenburg subject in a note handed in to the Electoral State Chancellery."

A highly effective moment, holding up the dénouement of the story. The reader recovers hope and even if Kohlhaas' entanglement in misdeeds gradually begins to appear even to him as guilt whose voluntary admission will in the end confirm the greatness of the man, the hope no longer applies to saving the person of Kohlhaas but to the victory of justice. A new apparatus is now involved, the Emperor, the Empire and now, when the lawyers are on their own and personal rancour and relationships are, or are made, ineffective, Kohlhaas' spirit is refined to a humility which is quite other than religious, namely the realization that, as the first sentences of the novella state with sublime terseness, he had "digressed into a virtue", the sense of justice. The individual case, the concrete fact in a situation of almost ludicrous simplicity — measured against the reaction — namely the fattening of the horses by Tronka, is seen in relation to the absolute; one might say that the fattening of the horses is a symbol of the absolute. It was for this that the horse-dealer resorted to arms, not as an incendiary but to show to what use arms may be put: the execution of "the" right. The idea was to make visible that sword carried before him on a crimson cushion, and Luther confirmed his right.

In his campaign for the right Kohlhaas overcomes war. Just as in *Penthesilea* the annihilation of the body makes the beauty of the soul visible, as Thusnelda's coquetry reveals the world of cunning, deceit and lies for what it is, having been a veil across her greatness, so in his misdeeds against citizens, Church and Prince, Kohlhaas had a higher cause which remains intact — but not altogether.

A certain Nagelschmidt appears, whom Kohlhaas had dismissed from his band for bad behaviour and this man, burning and murdering, represents himself as Kohlhaas' governor and actually offers him freedom through a messenger. Kohlhaas accepts. This is the direct cause of his condemnation. It is a similar fall before victory to the transformation of Agnes into Ottokar and Ottokar into Agnes, to the descent of Jupiter in the form of the Theban general. The Doppelgänger motif always appears in Kleist when the tension is too great and only the double nature of the phenomenon can demonstrate the greatness of the character. Kohlhaas' name and fame are so great that a street thief can exploit them to justify his existence. When Kohlhaas accepts Nagelschmidt's offer, which is put to him as a trap, this demonstrates his culpability in the eyes of the corrupt court of the councillors and princes — in fact he accepts it for the sake of his higher mission. Here we see once again the Kleistian tragic situation which is dialectically inverted because it is in conflict with its own reality. The episode changes nothing in his general fate, but it stresses once again, the intermingling of justice and injustice, guilt and freedom.

When Kohlhaas is already under the protection of Brandenburg, the Elector of Saxony, a foolish adorer of the Lady Heloise, floating in vacuous happiness, discovers that Kohlhaas is the only person from whom he could have obtained the answer to the secret of eternity, the problem of destiny. Kohlhaas has the gypsy's mysterious scrap of paper hanging round his neck.

"The Elector, with half-naked chest, his feathered hat adorned with pine needles in huntsman's fashion, sitting next to the Lady Heloise who had been his first love in the days of his early youth, said, made merry by the stimulus of the feast dancing about him: Let us go thither and give the unfortunate, whoe'er he be, this goblet of wine."

When the Elector discovers that the prisoner is Kohlhaas, he places the goblet "red through and through . . . on a dish held out to him by a page for this purpose at a sign from the chamberlain." This is the same Elector who promises a little later to release Kohlhaas from imprisonment in Brandenburg if he gives him that scrap of paper, but then it is "Kohlhaas, who rejoiced over the power given to him to deal a deadly wound to his enemy's heel at the very moment when it is treading him in the dust." So the Saxon — unworthy of true destiny and higher knowledge — is actually destroyed by the dying Kohlhaas: a tragic but complete victory.

The invention and introduction of the gypsy into the story is a parallel to that of Luther. The reformer was able to give Kohlhaas spiritual consolation, justification before God; but his spiritualism was unable to satisfy the earthly Kohlhaas, who did not wish to forgive the wicked Junker Wenzel: this is Kleist's criticism of the form of Christianity he knew. It repudiated the war waged bloodily for justice and encouraged Kohlhaas' submission to an authority which was an idol of justice and regarded a pretty masquerade as a foretaste of heaven. Kleist-Kohlhaas would have been ready for this Christianity; the moral integrity of the man Luther is beyond all doubt, but he lacked the unqualified character of something for which the gypsy is a symbol: destiny determined for all eternity, the secret of existence.

She stands for omniscience and possesses the key to the secret of omnipotent divinity: why the Elector of Saxony had to make himself the deadly enemy of the one person from whom he could learn his destiny and why he had to do nothing but wrong to Kohlhaas, who had put himself voluntarily in his hands in order to maintain his right. Here is the mystery of existence in the theological sense and it is profoundly significant that Kleist knew how inseparable from the secrets of the ego was the secret of the other; that one exists in relation to the other and that the common pivotal point is to be found in the endless return to eternal authorities. This is the meaning of Kohlhaas' appeal for justice: how can the right of the individual, which is felt to be absolute, be realized in this fragile and constitutionally unjust world? The answer is: justification through death.

"He joyfully assured the Arch-chancellor, standing and placing his hand on his bosom, that his highest wish on earth had been fulfilled; moved over to the horses, looked them over and patted their fleshy necks, and cheerfully told the Chancellor, as he returned to him, that he bestowed them on his two sons Heinrich and Leopold ... The Elector cried: 'Now, Kohlhaas, the horse-dealer, now that satisfaction has come to you in this way, prepare yourself for your part to give satisfaction to His Imperial Majesty, whose advocate is standing here, for breach of the peace of his land!' Kohlhaas, removing his hat and flinging it to the ground, said he was prepared to do so ..."

Then his head falls; Kleist reports it in a subordinate phrase.
Kohlhaas had previously "received the benefit of Holy Communion" from Luther's emissary. The gesture shows the discrepancy between the Kleistian and the Christian vision of the world. Even temptation comes to him once again. The gypsy promises him life and freedom if he wil leave her the fateful scrap of paper, but he refuses.

"The woman, setting her child on the ground, said that in many respects he was right and that he could do and leave alone what he liked! And with this she took her stick in hand again and was about to go. Kohlhaas repeated his question as to the

Berlin University (Engraving by Calau)

The Brandenburg Gate (Engraving by Hausheer after Schröder)

content of the wonderful paper; he wished, when she answered rapidly, that he actually could open it, although it was simply curiosity to obtain knowledge of a thousand other things before she left him: who she really was, whence she had gained the knowledge inherent in her, why she had refused the paper to the Elector, for whom it was actually written, and given it to him, out of so many thousands of people, when he had never desired her knowledge? — Now it happened that at this very moment a sound became audible, caused by some police officers coming up the steps, so that the woman, seized by sudden anxiety at being caught by them in these apartments, replied: 'So long, Kohlhaas, so long! You shall not, if we meet again, lack knowledge of all this!' And with this, as she turned to the door, she cried: 'Farewell, little children, farewell', kissed the small family in turn, and left."

He would not lack knowledge of all this! The whole dialogue, held in subjunctive form, as well as the belief, already disclosed to the reader, in probable improbabilities, cannot remove the powerful impression of the voice of destiny itself, the ultimate authority. What the gypsy says twice over: "Goodbye" to Kohlhaas and "Farewell" to the children, already refers to something beyond this earth and in another language, speaking to other senses, where no more knowledge is needed but everything is given as in sleep, in dream, in play, as a gift, in paradise. And of course we have to believe with Kleist, for "probability is not always on the side of the truth."

Narrative Media
(The Novellas)

We are told by Tieck that Kleist descended to narrative with gnashing of teeth, for he felt himself to be a dramatist and told the publishers that he was prepared to write a play a year.

Although Kleist's stories represent a peak of German prose, they are very distant from the plays: it is true that one can infer the dramatist from the symbols and problems of the tales, but not the converse. The tales speak differently, for in them it is not the characters who speak but the narrator who talks about them. For a writer whose characters are enigmas to themselves, this is very strange, because the omniscience of the narrator in relation to his characters contradicts the enigma. Kleist, the greatest of all psychologists, therefore very seldom, if ever, provides psychological explanations. He lets us guess what the characters are thinking or feeling. When Kohlhaas reads Luther's bill, he turns red — but he does not speak. Such a man's flush is more eloquent than his tongue.

All Kleist's plays are like trials. Jupiter interrogates Alkmene, the Vehmic Court interrogates Käthchen, Adam interrogates Evchen, Hohenzollern interrogates the Prince of Homburg, the Amazons interrogate Penthesilea and in *Schroffenstein*, the hostile parties interrogate one another through intermediaries. Part of the riddle is slowly unravelled in this way. In the novellas, Kleist tries to use similar media, but they are more difficult to apply because stories do not consist of tantalizing dialogues but of reports of actual events. The world is questionable, of course, and will be questioned, and that is how the contradictions come to light. This is relatively clear in *Michael Kohlhaas*. In the other stories more spheres overlap without corresponding; the truth is therefore very difficult to find.

By nature Kleist loved riddles and mysteries. The Marquise von O is pregnant and does not know how. The three iconoclasts in *St. Cecilia* are driven mad by church music. *The Foundling* contains a whole series of incredibly mysterious details. They make the world seem chaotic and from this madhouse Kleist draws the materials for his novellas. The material for Kohlhaas was in a national chronicle, that of the Duel in Froissart, the Marquise von O in Rousseau's *Nouvelle Héloïse*. Where the materials are drawn from the present, as in *Betrothal in San Domingo* (subsequently moved from the environment of the French Revolution to the Central American colonies), and *Earthquake in Chile,* Kleist's artistic imagination manages with great assurance to link together the arresting points in the wilderness of existence with lines and to weave a net. Everything which meant the outside world and fiction could have been trash, but Kleist does not get lost in the material. Of course, it is only on the basis of the total oeuvre that one can say what Kleist was trying to say through Littergarde in *The Duel,* through Jeronimo Rugera and Toni. The characters alone seem at first glance to be suffering a senseless fate in a senseless world.

The extraordinary situation creates the essence of the person in the novella, it has been said, and in this genre Kleist wrote the most powerful novellas of German literature. The human being in catastrophe, especially when he is the single individual, raised from the mass, feels himself a stranger in the world. The earthquake destroyed the city, but at the same time burst open the prison and convent of the lovers, so that in the general misfortune they find their fortune:

"By now the most beautiful night had fallen, full of a magically gentle fragrance, as silvery and still as only a poet might have dreamed it. All along the valley spring, people had settled down in the bright moonlight and were preparing soft couches of moss and leaves for themselves to rest on after that terrible day. And because the poor souls were still wailing: this one that he had lost his house, another his wife and child and the third, everything, Jeronimo and Josephe stole away to thicker undergrowth so that the secret rejoicing of their souls would trouble no one. They found a splendid pomegranate tree which spread its branches of fragrant fruit abroad; and in its crown the nightingale fluted his melodious song. Here Jeronimo sat against the trunk and Josephe on his, Philipp on Josephe's lap, covered by his coat, and rested. The shadow of the tree with its filtered light passed over them and the moon was already paling in the sunlight before they fell asleep. For

Heinrich von Kleist (crayon drawing by Wilhelmine von Zenge, 1806)

they had endless matter to talk of, the convent and the prisons and what they had suffered on each other's behalf; and they were very moved when they thought what misery had had to come upon the world to make them happy!"

In passages like these Kleist's language has calmed down, becoming simple, almost homely, and however rarely his work contains passages where the elect find heaven, their rarity merely corresponds to the ineffability of poetry. In the *Betrothal in San Domingo*, the most splendid of all Kleist's tales, all the external events are reflections of the philosophy slowly won from the plays. There is an almost effortless simplicity in reading off, through the mestiza Toni, who was used in the negro rising as a decoy for whites, a number of Kleistian experiences and questions, from the Doppelgänger bride, the beloved seen in a dream, the difference between the outward appearance and the inner essence, the mysterious origins, to the point of subjugation by an ideology blind to reality (racial hatred), love at first sight, sudden release, the night and then the death of love. We can see the stock-in-trade of Kleist's sensuality in detail: the pinafore, the washing, the make-believe, Toni's youth and the bed-scene, with the succinct sentence: "What more happened we need not report, because everyone who comes to this point reads it for himself." At the end we read:

"But a deep dream, of which she seemed to be the subject, preoccupied him: at least she heard repeatedly from his burning, trembling lips the whispered word: Toni! An indescribable melancholy seized her; she could not decide to wrest him back from a heaven of sweet fantasy into the depths of a mean and miserable reality; and in the certainty that sooner or later he must awaken of himself, she knelt at his bedside and covered his dear hand with kisses."

A passage like this acquires its full savour only in the scene under the elderbush in *Käthchen von Heilbronn*. Several times

110

The Lindenpromenade in Berlin about 1810

Kleist reproduced dramatic scenes epically in a related manner. The symbols, once found, were among the fixtures of his literary media.

The outward image is a symbol of the inner form. On it lies the brightness of the soul, a freshness which makes one seem to understand after reading it what the literary art is. How can the *sweet creature*, so often exemplarily represented in a weak and extremely young girl, escape the confusion into which the crude world casts her? Answer: by dreaming or being saved from the conscious sphere by removal to the unconscious.

Against all the painful certainty of her "case", the Marquise von O maintains her innocence and accordingly puts notices seeking the father of her child in the newspaper. She is as innocent as a character in fairy tale, spelling out riddles. And the strength of purity is so coercive that ultimately she uses the solution of the riddle to her own benefit, against her mother, father and the whole world. True, the alienation lasts a very long time, fills the whole tale and does not only torment the characters involved but also the reader, so that the tension becomes agonizing and strains the nerves. In the Marquise, however, the riddle is only solved in order to unleash a second. The Countess has already resigned herself to the idea that the huntsman is the child's father; then, when the Count, its real father, appears, she is so horrified that she refuses to marry him. She suddenly realises when it was that the Count must have overwhelmed her and is so astonished at this despicable act by a man she had taken for a man of honour that the solution is delayed until the last line of the tale: "He would not have appeared to her as a devil then, had he not appeared as an angel the first time she saw him."

Kleist exploits all the paradoxes of the situation with an energy which is almost rallying. This becomes ironically clear in *The Duel*, where the human and divine courts speak against Littergarde — until the truth comes to light when her protector Friedrich recovers from a fatal wounding and the slanderer and villain gradually declines from a slight infection. For Kleist, the pure human being stands in the centre of a cyclone. Himself unmoved, he sees the world torn to pieces. But suddenly he is distracted from within. A fire, a madness seizes him, to the point of possession. Such searing fires are Kohlhaas' sense of justice, eroticism in Toni and *The Foundling*, the power of music in *St. Cecilia*. The world suddenly becomes daemonic, threatening innocence with destruction. This kind of thing had previously only appeared in Shakespeare. In Kleist the core of the character is shaken, overthrown, falls and goes under, without having known moral guilt: only Kohlhaas and Homburg solve the riddles of their characters and gain serenity and freedom.

The "Berliner Abendblätter"

Kleist gained some succès d'estime with his tales. They were printed singly in journals and he then prepared a collected volume, which was to be published by Reimer in Berlin in 1810. He was given *Michael Kohlhaas,* the *Marquise von O* and *Earthquake in Chile.* These were the "moral tales" which were ready. But there were disappointments with the plays. Goethe condemned *Penthesilea, The Broken Jug* failed in Weimar, the *Warrior's Battle* could not be printed. Iffland's theatre in Berlin stubbornly closed its doors to him.

At the end of 1809 Kleist spent a short time in Frankfurt-an-der-Oder. He was still physically, spiritually and financially close to ruin. Almost impoverished, he went in 1810 to Berlin, where he is said to have offered his services to the king as an officer in vain. In Berlin he no longer moved in the circles of the nobility and officers, his one-time professional and social equals, but in circles where literature, theatre, music and Jewish capital mixed. Adam Müller seems to have introduced him into society this time as well. He was a guest at the Christian-German dinner circle. Here Kleist met Fouqué, Arnim, Brentano, Varnhagen and Rahel and the composer Bernhard Anselm Weber. Wilhelm Grimm was staying in Berlin as Arnim's guest. Loeben and the Eichendorff brothers were studying there.

In 1810 Brentano described the circle of his friends to Görres, saying of Kleist: "The Phoebus Kleist, whom Müller thought dead, had returned here from Prague and now that I have read the rest of his works scattered through Phoebus, especially the beginning of *Käthchen von Heilbronn* and the beautiful *Kohlhaas* tale, I was really delighted to know him alive and to see him. He is a gentle, serious man of thirty-two, of about my height; his last tragedy, Arminius, cannot be printed because it is too applicable to our time; he was an officer and Kammerassessor, but cannot stop writing and is, accordingly, poor."

On 1 October 1810 a new newspaper appeared in Berlin under the title *Berliner Abendblätter*. It was a journalistic novelty in that it appeared daily — apart from Sundays — in the evening and was the first newspaper to carry the police reports issued in the afternoon, that is news of crimes, murder, fire and accidents. It was a sensational paper for popular circulation. The arrival of the newspaper was announced in good time on the street corners of Berlin and advertisements and other notices appeared in other papers. The paper contained four pages of print and was in the octavo format, which was as unusual for papers then as it is now, being book-size. The first issue was printed in huge numbers and distributed free of charge. The unnamed editor was Heinrich von Kleist.

The format, the daily publication, the evening appearance were uncommon and liable to arouse interest. Advertising by posters and free handouts was a sensation in those days. The *Abendblätter* were most astonishing of all because they published police reports. Kleist owed this to personal acquaintance with the Police Directorate, whose President, Gruner, was a friend of his. When the police reports became more scanty later on, the Editor supplemented the topical side of his paper with a bulletin of news items from foreign papers. He wanted to include political news, but could not get permission from the State Chancellery (under Hardenberg). At that time there were no daily papers in Berlin; only Nuremberg and Stuttgart could boast such achievements. The Hamburg papers appeared four times a week, the Berlin ones — the Voss and Spener papers — three times. Advertisements appeared only in the so-called intelligence sheets; there was one in Berlin which appeared daily. Entertaining reports and contributions, about science and the arts, were not at first within Kleist's aims — he wanted to affect broad circles, the large, metropolitan public; it was at these that the police and sensational news were aimed, so literature and politics were excluded in favour of information. The cultural side was taken into account first of all in the form of theatre reviews only — here a sarcastic attitude towards the

Clemens Brentano (1788—1842)

Friederike (Rahel) Varnhagen von Ense
(Drawing by Wilhelm Hensel, 1822)

national theatre and Iffland were speedily visible. Some such contributions were signed H. v. K. and A. v. M.; so that readers could soon assume that these initials stood for the editorial board.

The police items flowed less freely as time passed, and not at all after Gruner's dismissal, to the great chagrin of readers and editors alike. Their place was taken by entertaining contributions and reports on foreign papers. Just as Kleist's sensational and theatrical reviews from Berlin were soon copied by other papers, usually with attributions, so he too adopted contributions from other papers. Great local interest was aroused by the *town news,* which might report on the unsuccessful balloon flight of a Berlin oil-cloth manufacturer. People were very interested in flight and a special article on *aeronautics* actually once appeared in the *Berliner Abendblätter.*

The paper was tremendously popular. An imitation was soon brought out in Hamburg, the *Beobachter an der Spree,* and in November 1810 the weekly Berlin scandal-sheet of Ernst Litfass, later to become famous for his advertising pillars, brought out a parody of Kleist's paper under the title *Excerpts from the Extraordinary Small-town Daily.* But by the beginning of December sales were falling off appreciably. Hitzig stopped publishing the paper and Kleist sought and found a new publisher in August Kuhn; but "the actual evening papers, as originally planned by Kleist, ceased on 22 December with paper 72" (Sembdner).

The reasons for the failure of the initially welcomed papers were not political, although the first objections arose over the reportage of the Spanish War of Independence and Adam Müller's popular glosses aroused the disapproval of the authorities. The true reason for its failure was simply that after the police reports stopped, the rest of the material in the paper was not sufficently attractive. State Chancellor Hardenberg saw this clearly when Kleist turned to him with a complaint. The public was principally interested in murders, robberies, frauds and fires and turned away in disappointment as soon as Kleist had

116

Extrablatt
zum 7ten Berliner Abendblatt.

Polizeiliche Tages=Mittheilungen,

Etwas über den Delinquenten Schwarz
und die Mordbrenner=Bande.

Die Verhaftung des in den Zeitungen vom 6. d. M.
signalisirten Delinquenten Schwarz (derselbe unge=
nannte Vagabonde, von dem im isten Stück dieser
Blätter die Rede war) ist einem sehr unbedeutend
scheinenden Zufall zu verdanken.

Nachdem er sich bei dem Brande in Schönberg
die Taschen mit gestohlnem Gute gefüllt hatte, ging
er sorglos, eine Pfeife in der Hand haltend, durch
das Potsdamsche Thor in die Stadt hinein. Zufällig
war ein Soldat auf der Wache, welcher bei dem Krü=
ger La Bal in Steglitz gearbeitet hatte, und die Pfeife
des Schwarz als ein Eigenthum des La Bal erkannte.

Dieser Umstand gab Veranlassung, den Schwarz
anzuhalten, näher zu examiniren, und nach Schönberg
zum Verhör zurückzuführen, wo sich denn mehrere,
dem re La Bal und dem Schulzen Willmann in Schön=
berg gehörige, Sachen bei ihm fanden.

Bei diesem ersten Verhöre in Schönberg standen,
wie sich nachher ergeben hat, mehrere seiner Spieß=
gesellen vor dem Fenster, und gaben ihm Winke und
verabredete Zeichen, wie er sich zu benehmen habe.
Dieses Verhör wurde während des ersten Tumults
gehalten, wie der Brand noch nicht einmal völlig
gelöscht war, und niemand konnte damals schon ahn=
den, mit welchem gefährlichen Verbrecher man zu
thun habe.

Special sheet of the "Berliner Abendblätter", 1810

117

to adopt reports from elsewhere. The local attraction was lost and the literary contributions which make Kleist's enterprise important to us were of no interest to the public at large. The *Abendblätter* published several of Kleist's finest essays and stories, his anecdotes, the *Up-to-date Plan of Education,* the *Prayer of Zoroaster,* the *Beggar-woman of Locarno, St. Cecilia* and the essay on the *Puppet Theatre.* Kleist found the material for the anecdotes in papers and calendars, but he gave them both their telling point and their stylistic colour.

Many of these anecdotes are genuine short stories: *The Mischief of Heaven, The New (Happier) Werther, The Strange Story in Italy* and *The Improbable Veracities.* They display Kleist's sense of wit and bluff and his striking and ingenious formulation. At the same time, writing these stories down quickly for the newspaper, he became aware of the unique

Freiherr von Hardenberg (Engraving by F. Bolt, 1815)

118

Mauerstrasse with the Church of the Holy Trinity in Berlin

nature of the genre; Kleist realised that the formula was effective by means of those nuances he gave to the incidents, the moment of suspense, working up to the surprise with an unexpected conclusion. His mastery in this field can be clearly seen through a comparison with another German anecdotist, Johann Peter Hebel. Both authors told the following anecdote, probably drawing on the same source. Hebel:

Poor Wages

In the last war when the Frenchmen came to Berlin, to the city of residence of the King of Prussia, much royal property was taken and driven away or sold. For war gives nothing, it takes. However well-hidden it was, everything was discovered and much of it looted; but not all. A large supply of royal building wood long remained unbetrayed and intact. But at last yet another rogue among the King's own subjects came along and thought, there's good money to be made here, and he showed the French commandant, with many a smirk and

119

roguish look, what a fine stack of oak and pine timbers were laid together, here and here, from which many thousands of guilders could be made. But the good commandant gave him poor thanks for his treachery, saying: "Let the fine timber lie where it is, one must not take the necessities of life from the enemy. For if your King comes back he will need wood for new gallows for such honest subjects as you."

A vigorous story, told without bitterness and with the moral arising so innocently that it has gone into children's reading books. The expressions "rogue" und "smirk" mitigate the meanness, rather than arousing indignation. Hebel is not trying to awaken patriotic fury but aims at moral instruction, intended to shame. With Kleist it is otherwise:

French Fairness
(Fit to be graven on brass)

During the war a citizen came to the French General Hulin and reported, for the purpose of seizure under martial law for the benefit of the enemy, a number of timbers lying in the pontoon yard. The General, who was just dressing, said: "No, my friend; we cannot take this timber." "Why not?" asked the citizen, "it is royal property." "That is why," said the General, taking a quick look at him. "The King of Prussia needs that kind of timber, to have such villains hanged on it as you."

Kleist's version is much more concrete; the French general is mentioned by name, the scene, which is set very skillfully with all the details ("who was just dressing", "taking a quick look at him"), is entirely focussed on the general's answer. Hebel's narrative intimacy has gone, gone also is the cosy tone. On the contrary, the strikingly sharp contrast between the "villain" and the decent officer is expressed in the general's contemptuous terseness. The subject is not the general himself but the condemnation of the villain. The anecdote's few lines contain

120

Achim von Arnim (1781—1831) Painting by Ströhling

Friedrich Baron de la Motte-Fouqué (1777—1843)
Painting by Wilhelm Hensel, 1818

the psychological sketch of a miserable subject who feels impelled to cast himself on the enemy's neck. The intensity of the judgement is all the more annihilating spoken by the enemy with whom the man is trying to ingratiate himself. Whereas Hebel caught only the moral despicability of such an act and set it down instructively as a deterrent example, Kleist builds from words and phrases a dramatic scene of satirical impact, because for him, who believed that the nobility of the human being, his "vocation", was identical with the divine, a deed such as this must express the absolute worthlessness of the doer.

A large number of the "fellow-eaters" (Mitesser) as Brentano called the Dining Society, collaborated in Kleist's *Abendblätter*. After dinner they would sit over a pipe of tobacco chatting (Kleist was a great pipe smoker; his pipe seems never to have grown cold). They were neither Brandenburgers nor Junkers, but mainly writers, students, men of letters, painters and journalists, an artistic circle. The fact that a good many of these men were or became soldiers seems obvious when one remembers that for fifteen years Napoleon had been keeping

August Wilhelm Iffland (1759—1814), actor and producer

the European world busy fighting. Almost all were impoverished and even the wealthy, like Arnim, had had to lower their standard of living. Of course politics were also discussed; Fouqué and Kleist, as trained military men, liked discussing military matters — not for the pleasure of the craft but because it was an area where they were in harmony. There had to be a break with Brentano because he was offended by Kleist's independent alterations of his and Arnim's dialogue *Feelings Before Friedrich's Seascape*. The most faithful collaborator was Fouqué, who in any case knew exactly how much Kleist's economic existence depended on the continuation of the *Abendblätter*. Arnim's verdict on Kleist (to Wilhelm Grimm, April 1810), is remarkable: "After Fouqué, Kleist arrived, a slightly perverted character as is almost always the case when talent has emerged from the old Prussian settings. He is the most uninhibited, almost cynical man I have met for a long time, has a certain uncertainty of speech, close to a stammer, and expresses himself in his work by constant deletions and alterations. He lives very curiously, often spending whole days in bed, in order to work away unmolested at his pipe of tobacco."

This was also the year of Kleist's collision with Iffland, Director of the Berlin Theatre. Kleist had sent him *Käthchen von Heilbronn* for performance. For a long time there was no answer, but Kleist wanted to make Iffland declare himself and therefore asked him to return the manuscript, as he needed it for a few days. Iffland sent off the manuscript at once and that very evening Kleist heard that the omnipotent man of the theatre had said he didn't like *Käthchen* and what he did not like he would not perform. At this Kleist wrote his ferocious note of 12 August 1810:

"Sir,
You have returned to me, through Herr Römer, the play performed at the Vienna theatre on the occasion of the nuptual celebrations, Käthchen von Heilbronn, with the remark that

you do not like it. I am sorry, to tell the truth, that it is a girl; had it been a boy it would probably have appealed to you more, Sir.

I am, Sir, yours faithfully,
Heinrich von Kleist."

The Puppet Theatre

It is true, and the evidence affirms that none of his friends and acquaintances knew what Kleist was. This may be sad, and contributed to the fact that in the end he called his life the most agonising that a man had led. But it seems to be no less true that he himself never really knew himself; he remained an enigma to himself. And yet in his last year he must have come upon insights and discoveries of such an enormously strange and at the same time encouraging nature, that he should have got on the trail of himself and his fate. There are hints of this in *Michael Kohlhaas*, the *Warrior's Battle* and the *Prince of Homburg*. If one could lay bare the bones of the statements made through his style and the speaking characters, one would see the mysterious point at which they come together and from which they were nourished.

Discoursing, narrating — in those very months — he succeeded just once in making the riddle of existence comprehensible to such an extent that the viewer shrinks from the vision. These are the insights of a rider across Lake Constance: for a moment the merciful shell which has hidden the truth falls away and, dazzled with the superabundance of light, one is thrown to the ground. In the essay *On The Puppet Theatre*, Kleist reached this point.

The central motif of his writing is grasped in the symbol of the puppet. The incongruity of dream-truth and world deception, of the divine feeling of I and the disdainful strangeness of this I in the world is clearly seen to be the problem of his life.

Kleist's struggles consisted for the most part in efforts to be clear about himself. That stage is now reached. Penthesilea's desperate state of darkness is revealed as a stage on the road; even Käthchen's certainty of faith is a stage — whereas it is only the late Kohlhaas and then the Prince of Homburg who teach both: darkness to the brink of the grave and then, from the experience of death, a brightness which was Kleist's own experience. His own death was extravagantly celebrated by him as a decisive step towards understanding and knowledge.

In the article *On the Puppet Theatre* the stages of this modern Via Dolorosa are described as stages of consciousness. First the natural, naïve charm of the puppet moved by wires, which has a centre of gravity outside itself. From here consideration moves to the "disturbances" of consciousness by deliberation (Pulling out the Thorn) and on to the healthy "consciousness" of the struggling bear, debouching finally in the reference to the conquest of the original sin in paradise. There is much to remind us of Romantic psychology and its mythological metaphysics, still more of the Christian doctrine of vindication and grace; such associations will no doubt have helped Kleist to articulate his "system" — but at bottom, the pattern was neither Romantic nor Christian but a Gnostic doctrine of self-redemption.

For a long time Kohlhaas and the Prince of Homburg were blind. The law which condemned both to death, the law of the state and the law of war, lies outside their own focus; they do not recognise it and therefore they cannot respect it. That is why Homburg interprets the Elector's thoughts and actions wrongly. Penthesilea's love for Achilles is irritated to madness by the conventional national consciousness. Käthchen is thought a witch because, contrary to custom and reason, she runs after her love. Penthesilea and Käthchen remain in their world and each obtains justice in her way. Kohlhaas and the Prince experience the crisis of realization. The "focus", their feeling of divinity, shifts and now they recognise their blindness, or rather, folly.

125

But the essay *On the Puppet Theatre* does not discuss the formal structure of the plays, in abstract form as it were, but sees the problem as a metaphor and illustration. Misleading as it may be to interpret Kleist's work on the basis of this essay, the problems which arise are difficult, for each of the plays is infinitely more than the realisation of feelings and ideas, namely creation from a law of his own. Each play sets a human being with his own system in the world, where he wants to see himself for what he is. The process is so difficult because he does not know exactly what the world is. Hence these comic or tragic dénouements. One of the causes of such confusion is made surprisingly clear in *The Puppet Theatre:*

"I enquired about the mechanism of these figures and how it was possible to control their individual limbs and joints without having a myriad threads on one's fingers, as demanded by the rhythm of the movements, or the dance.

He replied that I should not imagine that every limb was individually placed and pulled by the operator at the various moments of the dance.

Every movement, he said, had its centre of gravity; it was enough to control this, within the figure; the limbs, which were not like pendulums, followed of themselves mechanically without any assistance . . .

I asked him if he thought that the operator controlling these puppets should himself be a dancer, or at least have a concept of the beauty of the dance?

He replied that if a business was easy from the mechanical aspect, that did not mean that it could be run quite without feeling.

The line which had to be described by the centre of gravity was certainly very simple and, as he thought, in most cases straight. In cases where it was curved, the law of its curve seemed to be at least of the first or at most of the second degree; and even in this last case only elliptical, a form which was completely natural to the movement of the extremities of the

Puppet

human body (owing to the joints) and it was therefore no great art for the operator to register it.

On the other hand, from another aspect, this line was something very mysterious. For it was no less than the *way of the dancer's soul;* and he doubted that it could be found other than by the operator transposing himself into the centre of gravity of the puppet, in other words, *dancing.*

I replied that the business had been described to me as something rather spiritless; something like the turning of the crank-handle to play the barrel-organ.

By no means, he said. Rather, the movement of his fingers related quite artistically to the movement of the puppets attached to them, rather as numbers to their logarithms, or asymptote to hyperbole . . ."

We must remember that even as a lieutenant Kleist had studied mathematics in Potsdam, and mechanics, physics and chemistry interested him: here is their echo after almost ten years. It cannot be an accident that in this essay Kleist takes his main metaphor from mechanics, a science which led to the discovery of the quantum of effect. One is tempted to say that in his work Kleist had already shown how analysis encounters final acts which do not fundamentally stand up to analysis, where one has to "believe". That is why he called the final certainty of the ego a *divine* one. To construct a puppet so that balance, lightness and mobility were ideal would mean that it would have the advantage over living dancers of never being able to put on airs: "for, as you know, affectation arises when the soul (vis motrix) is in some other place than the centre of gravity of the movement."

"Additionally, he said, these puppets have the advantage that they possess antigravity. They know nothing of the inertia of matter, that property most inimical to the dance; because the strength which lifts them in the air is greater than that which binds them to the earth. What would our good G . . . give to be 60 lbs lighter, or to have a weight of this magnitude helping her to perform her entrechats and pirouettes? The puppets only need the ground, like elves, in order to *brush* it and revive the impetus of their limbs by means of the momentary inhibition; we need it to *rest* on and to recover from the exertion of the dance: an element which is obviously not a dance itself and with which nothing more can be done than to make it disappear, if possible.

I said that however skilfully he pleaded the cause of his paradox, he would never make me believe that there could be more charm contained in a mechanical mannikin than in the structure of the human body. He retorted that it was simply impossible for a human being even to catch up with the mannikin in this respect. Only a god could match matter in this area; and this was the point where the two ends of the circular world met.

I was more and more astonished and did not know what to say to such extraordinary assertions.

It seemed, he replied, taking a pinch of tobacco, that I had not read the third chapter of Genesis with attention; and one could not very well talk about the succeeding ones, still less of the last, with a man who did not know this first period of all human civilization.

I said that I would be very glad to know what disorders in the natural grace of the human being consciousness brings about . . ."

Here follows the episode of the young man who wants to imitate the grace of the boy pulling out the thorn before the mirror; but the attempt fails, becomes comic, in fact.

A whole series of matters central to Kleist are touched on: the body, the paradox of consciousness, grace and charm, nature (Rousseau's old magic formula), the parallel between the puppet and God, the Amphitryon theme and finally the rich image of the meeting point of the "circular world", which must of course be explained by Kleist's idea of the history of the world and not by cosmic geometry: according to Kleist, man's path runs in a straight line from paradise and paradise is its goal. This is the subject of the last section of the essay.

Here he tells the story of the bear which is more able than any human being to parry all the blows of a swordsman. He does not even bother with feints, but standing eye to eye, as though he could read his adversary's soul therein, he lifts his paws to strike and does not move when the blows are not to be taken seriously. Then the essay concludes:

129

"Now, my excellent friend, said Herr C . . ., you are in possession of everything which is necessary in order to understand me. We see that to the extent to which, in the organic world, the reflection becomes darker and weaker, the grace in it emerges ever more brilliantly and dominantly. — But just as the intersection of two lines on one side of a point, after the transition through the infinite, suddenly occurs again on the other side, or the image of the concave glass, after it has travelled away into the infinite, suddenly reappears just in front of us: So also, when knowledge has, as it were, passed through an infinity, grace reappears; so that, at the same time, it appears at its purest in that human physical structure which has either no consciousness at all or an infinite one, i. e. in the puppet or in the god.

So then, I said rather distractedly, must we eat again from the Tree of Knowledge in order to fall back into the state of innocence?

Of course, he replied; that is the last chapter of the history of the world."

Is knowledge a betrayal? And if so, a betrayal of art in particular? Was it really Kleist's ideal to create art in a dream? Then what is the meaning of that *eating again* from the Tree of Knowledge? The other agrees, but this is to be the *last* chapter in the history of the world. Kohlhaas and the Prince of Homburg have this experience behind them. They have experienced the peace between spirit and matter, the ego and the world, and it is a peace of which only the naïve assume that it is bestowed. For them the soul is no longer a prisoner of the body, the Eternal is there at every moment. No more myths are needed, neither the invented one about the broken jug nor an historic one as in the Amazon play. One needs only oneself in the concrete situation, which is an absolute, indeed an eternal one.

The Prince of Homburg

The Prince of Homburg became known through Tieck, when he read the play at his famous recital evenings. Tieck boasted that he had done most to promote Kleist's fame thereby. For further generations he promoted Kleist's fame by publishing the play, which might otherwise have been lost, as were so many of Kleist's manuscripts. [1]

As early as 1816, Ferdinand Grimm informed his brothers Wilhelm and Jacob that a previously unknown play by the late Kleist was to be printed, but this did not actually happen until 1821. In the same year the play was produced at theatres in Vienna, Breslau, Frankfurt-am-Main, Dresden and a number of smaller places: Hamburg followed in 1823, Berlin not until 1828. The resistance came from Court and military circles. In Vienna Archduke Charles protested, in Berlin Duke Charles of Mecklenburg, brother of Queen Luise. Heinrich Heine wrote: "It is now decided that the Kleist play, *The Prince of Homburg*, is not to appear on our stages because, as I learn, a noble lady thinks that her ancestor appears in it in ignoble form. This play is still the Apple of Discord in our aesthetic societies. As far as I am concerned, I vote that it was, so to speak, written by the genius of poetry itself." The noble lady was Princess Wilhelm, Amalie Marianne, a native of Homburg.

The play opens in Fehrbellin, in a garden in the old French style. There is a castle in the background, with a slope leading down from it. It is night, the Prince, a Prussian cavalry general, is sitting, bareheaded and openshirted, half-waking, half-sleeping, under an oak tree, binding himself a wreath. The Elector of

---

[1] Lost pieces include *The Story of My Soul, The Idea Store* and *The Diary.* (It is probable that the three titles all refer to a single work.) *The Story of My Soul,* originally composed for Rühle von Lilienstern, was in the possession of Sophie von Haza, who married Adam Müller in 1809. In 1816 the daughter did not know what had happened to the manuscript. Presumably it was lost by a publisher.

Horst Caspar in the title role of Kleist's "Prinz von Homburg"

Brandenburg, his wife, his niece Natalie and others come secretly out of the castle and look down on him from the parapet of the slope. Pages with torches — this is the scene of the first act. The political and military situation is urgently in need of solution, the final battle with the Swedes, pursued for three days, is about to take place.

The Brandenburg troops have beaten the Swedes. The Great Elector, the victor, wants the Swedes to be pursued and has appointed the regiments under his General of Cavalry, the Prince of Homburg, to do it. The troops are to rest for three hours to feed the horses, and then continue. When the cavalry is already mounted and waiting for the Prince to place himself at their head, Homburg is found sleeping on a seat in the park, his fingers busy making a laurel-wreath like a sleepwalker, dreaming, seduced by the moonlight. The Prussian officers stare at him in astonishment as he sits there in his open white shirt. The Prince is dreaming of his love for a lady of the Court, Princess Natalie of Orange, a niece of the Elector.

The dreaming hero — Kleist's basic motif, the cavalry general as a sleepwalker, the war hero as lover! The warlike scene with stamping of hooves and trumpets yields to the image of a summer night filled with sweet fragrance, which in turn becomes the erotic image of the bride: Homburg dreams that he has laid himself down to rest in the lap of the Night Princess with her fair curls ("all dripping with fragrance"). The soldier play is a dream play: all the acts are bracketed by dream scenes. The reality of the dream reveals the truth of the heart. Here we are not helped by reference to the depth of the unconscious discovered by the Romantics, the phallic symbolism of sweet-scented flowers or the chain of allegorically disguised repressions. Heine is quite right when he says that the play is as it were "written by the genius of poetry itself". It happens, as in many of Shakespeare's or Calderon's plays, where ghosts and angels appear, without disturbing us. In Kleist they do not appear; everything takes place, always close to catastrophe, in the belief in love, truth and happiness.

133

The Prince is sleeping in the garden. The cavalry leaves without him. When Count Hohenzollern, his friend, calls him, he collapses *as if a bullet had struck him.* He returns laboriously to reality and no longer knows what he has thought or said in his dream. As they go he picks up a glove. It is Natalie's glove and now for the first time he remembers his fairy-tale dream. But he does not know who the girl in it was. The name has gone from him. In the next scene the Elector appears, founder of the New Prussia, commander and thinker, a magnificent personality. His faithful officers surround him. The ladies too are in the camp, among them Natalie. She misses her glove and as the Elector explains the situation to his officers and plans the battle, the still distracted Prince of Homburg notices that the Princess is looking for her glove and is able to slip it over to her. Suddenly, *as if struck by lightning* he realises that Natalie was the lady of whom he had dreamed.

In this exposition, the scenes of greatest genius in German drama, the development of the Prince and the character of the Elector are outlined. The battle takes place. Against the express orders of the Elector, the Prince attacks prematurely and is therefore liable, according to martial law, to the death sentence — although his premature action decided the Prussian victory. The Elector himself is placed in extreme danger and believed dead. The Prince, the victor, meets Natalie; the lovers find one another on the battlefield itself. Grief for the dead Elector and the happiness of love contradict one another. The Prince embraces Natalie, saying:

"Oh my sweet friend! If but this hour
Were not the hour of grief, then I would say:
Entwine your branches here about this breast."

Then it turns out that the Elector is alive. Characteristically, their senses have deceived them: it was not the Elector, but the equerry who had changed horses with him, who was riding the fallen white horse. (Here Kleist is weaving one of the prettiest

134

Gérard Philipe in a performance of "Der Prinz von Homburg"

Hohenzollern family legends into the story.) In the next scene, now in Berlin, the Elector reappears as the great lord, combining the state and private spheres within him, as senior politician and warm, feeling human being. Without knowing who is guilty he pronounces the verdict: whoever it was who led the cavalry and allowed the enemy to escape before the bridges could be destroyed owing to his premature assault, he would court martial: "he was guilty of death."

The court martial takes place. The verdict is death. The Elector signs. The Prince can hardly believe it. Surely, the Elector must pardon him? Is not he, the Prince, the victor of Fehrbellin? The Elector is subject to the law of reasons of state. When the Prince realises that the death-sentence must be carried out he is gripped by despair and fear of death. He pleads for his life. Kleist articulates the despair and fear of death here in verses of effulgent melancholy, in sharp contrast to the heroic and soldierly ideal of the age and its rhetoric. One would have to go a long way back, to antiquity, to Achilles' lament in the Underworld in Homer, to find a similarly profound appeal for naked life.

But from downfall comes liberation. When the Elector realises that the Prince has accepted the verdict and death, placing the law of the state above the ego, he can make use of the pardon, that pardon which transcends the execution of the sentence. But Homburg does not want a pardon! There is almost a mutiny when the troops march on the Elector's castle and request General Kottwitz to pardon the Prince in the name of the soldiers. The Elector has the Prince taken from prison and tells Kottwitz:
"He will instruct you, that I promise you, in martial discipline and obedience . . ."

The Prince declares that he wishes to die, he submits to the law. He is led to his death, or so he thinks when his eyes have been bound. He comes to that park where he had been dreaming at the start. Once again, in the fragrance of the damask

violets, he falls into his somnambulistic state, saying to Captain Stranz of the cavalry:
"Ah, how sweet the damask violets smell!
Do you not sense it?"

Stranz replies:
"They are gillifowers and sweet william . . .
It seems a maiden has been planting flowers here:
Shall I give you a flower?"

The Prince: "Dear friend!
I'll give them water when I am at home."

The Prince is "absent" to such an extent that he is not aware of the reality: he is prepared for death, but meanwhile the Elector has pardoned him.

The triumph of the Prussian legend, the fairy-tale, follows. the Elector — himself a character gradually revealed in the play — crowns him with the laurels which signify victory both as general and as poet. Cannonfire and music resound, the castle lights up, the officers hail the victor (who only a short time before has been assured that his name would be proclaimed from the pulpits as victor, even if he were to be shot: this is part of the Officers' Code). Is this opera a dream? Kottwitz says so: "A dream, what else?" and it is allowed to end in the cry: "May all the enemies of Brandenburg come to dust!"

Why can it do this? Because the legend, the fairytale, know in advance that it will end happily. The first scene has resolved "in a dream" the riddle whose unravelling has been the subject of the action. Beginning and end are almost silent pantomimes of a subject which is actually inexpressible, because to express is to destroy it. In *The Prince of Homburg,* the Prussian is the inexpressible. What is left of the story, which is "cyclical", is the touching of poles outside space and time. It becomes an event in literature, as literature. For only literature can present the tormenting ambivalence, in the person and the event, which is excluded from the discursive legend. Accordingly, the writer of this play has become the greatest writer of the Prussian Ideal, although as a man he stood far removed from it.

While the Prince believes himself dead, having looked into his grave, he has overcome the earthly aspect, not like one of Schiller's heroes, by an elevation of the will but by humiliation, by the counter-image of the coward he never was in battle. Whence the strength for this conquest came is never revealed. Kleist's monologues are short, even the Prince never speaks more than eleven lines; they express the shame of the solitary man who knows that no man exists who can understand the depths of his feeling. Here Kleist is connected with his hero, hence it is here, where the hero faces the Prussian State, that the solution of the poetic problem lies. True, it is just as secret as the hero, only the symbol of the laurel wreath and the pantomimic speechlessness of the character indicate it. It lies at a level where there is no more talking, where people feel, are pure, are divine. Kleist's poetic essence found peace in a state which is a literary exaltation into the legend, the fairy-tale. The Prussian State which Homburg and Kleist want does exist — more actually than any concrete form of Prussia — as an idea within them. The events of the world will obey this sense within because it is stronger than the world.

In *The Prince of Homburg* Kleist has solved his riddle. The dense, grammatically fragmented speech, its tumult and expressive form, are for him means of setting forth the "inexpressible man" as he called himself, at least in stumbling fashion. He has no hope that his own character will be understood. The reception of the play is the historical proof of how right he was. That is why *The Prince of Homburg* was his last play. Like Homburg, Kleist went through death and hoped for another life in paradise. In his last letter to Sophie von Haza-Müller he writes: "We . . . dream of purely heavenly fields and suns, in whose radiance we will wander up and down with long wings on our shoulders." Is this the immortality which the Prince had welcomed with such rejoicing? Kleist believed so.

The End on the Wannsee

In December 1810 the *Berliner Abendblätter* had lost so many subscribers that Kleist had his back to the wall. He tried to alter the character of the paper by making it into a kind of official gazette and asking men of the administrative bureacracy to write contributions. For this he expected a subsidy from the State Chancellery which was not forthcoming. In the spring of 1811 the paper ceased publication and Kleist, having lost a small pension from Queen Luise's private purse on her death, was threatened with complete penury. In various letters to Raumer and Hardenberg he tried to obtain a small pension from the State which had been promised him verbally. He now regarded the failure of the *Abendblätter* with bitterness, as the result of intrigues and censorship.

Ulrike seems to have helped with small supplements and now and again modest fees arrived from Reimer the publisher. The political situation was coming to a head and Kleist tried to return to the Prussian army, hoping to be of use on the King's staff, or at least as a company leader. Adam Müller left Berlin and Kleist became friendly with Fouqué, who invited him home, but in particular with his married cousin Marie von Kleist, with whom he had been on a friendly footing since the Potsdam days.

Marie was now a lady of 50 and faced with divorce (she was the innocent party in her divorce from Major Friedrich Wilhelm Christian von Kleist in 1812). She was the recipient of his last letters, his confidante, after Ulrike had dropped her brother under the influence of the Frankfurt relations, a woman to whom he could express his feelings on himself and his art; in the final months he used the familiar *Du* in his letters to her. He could confide to her that after the dejection of those months he would like to abandon art altogether and occupy himself with nothing but music, in addition to the sciences in which he still had some time to make up.

"For I regard this art as the root, or rather, to express myself in due form, as the algebraic formula of all others, and thus, as we already have a poet — with whom incidentally I would in no way venture to compare myself — who has referred all his ideas on the art he practises to colours, so I have from my earliest youth referred to music all the generalities I have thought about the art of writing. I believe that the thorough-bass contains the most important revelation on the art of writing." (May 1811, to Marie von Kleist)

Once again it looked as if everything might take a turn for the better. The King pardoned Kleist, he entered into a personal relationship with Gneisenau and associated with Rahel Levin.

Through Adam Müller Kleist met Henriette Vogel, the wife of one of the royal treasurers. He played music with her. She was suffering from a severe disease, probably cancer of the womb, and when she discovered through her doctor's negligence that her condition was hopeless she gave up. When Kleist once spoke, half-jestingly, half-moodily of shooting himself (he had also offered double suicide to Marie von Kleist), the word fell like a crystal into a lye bath. Everything in her attached itself to this idea, and Kleist, who revered Henriette but was not her lover, stirred her to intoxicated enthusiasm over the common "splendid grave" which would receive them. At last he had found his partner in death. Everything was carefully prepared and put into operation according to plan. On 9 November 1811 he wrote to Marie:

"My dearest Marie, in the midst of the paean of triumph which my soul is sounding in this moment of death, I must think of you yet again and explain myself to you as well as I can: to you, the only one whose feelings and opinion matter to me; all else on earth, both whole and in detail, I have fully overcome in my heart. Yes, it is true, I have gone behind your back, or rather I have gone behind my own; however, as I have told you a thousand times that I would not survive this, so now

Henriette Vogel

as I take my leave of you I give you the proof of it. During your stay in Berlin I exchanged you for another sweetheart; but, if this is any consolation to you, not for one to live with me, but for one who wishes to die with me, in the consciousness that I would be as unfaithful to her as to you. My relationship with this woman does not allow me to tell you more. Know only this, that my soul has become ripe for death through its contact with her own; that I have measured the whole glory of the human spirit against hers and that I die because there is nothing left on earth for me to learn or to acquire. Farewell! You are the single soul on earth whom I would wish to see again on the other side. What of Ulrike? — Yes, no, no, yes: it must depend on her own feelings. She has, methinks, not understood the art of sacrificing herself wholly, of going to the very end for what one loves: the most blessed thing that can be conceived of on earth, aye, what heaven must consist of, if it is true that one is glad and joyous there. Adieu!"

The next day he wrote to her once again:

"Your letters have split my heart asunder, my dearest Marie and had it been in my power, I assure you that I would have abandoned the decision I have taken to die. But I swear to you that it is quite impossible for me to live any longer; my soul is so stricken that I would almost say when I put my nose out of the window the daylight shining on it hurts me. Many would take this for sickness and exaggeration; but not you, who are capable of seeing the world from other standpoints than your own. Since I have had incessant traffic with beauty and morality since my earliest youth, in my thoughts and writings, I have become so sensitive that the slightest attack to which the feelings of every human being here below are exposed in the course of things, gives double and treble pain. So I assure you, I would rather suffer death ten times over than live again through what I felt last time in Frankfurt at the dinner table between my two sisters, especially when old Wackern arrived; get Ulrike to tell you about it some time. I have always loved my family from my heart, partly because of their goodnatured characters, partly because of the friendship they had for me; however little I may have spoken of it, so certain is it that it was one of my heartiest and inmost wishes to give them much happiness and honour one day through my work and books. Now, it is certainly true that in recent times it has in many respects been dangerous to be involved with me and I am all the less ready to accuse them of having withdrawn themselves from me, the more I consider the needs of the whole, which in part also rested on their shoulders; but the thought of seeing that merit which, after all, I have, be it large or small, going quite unrecognized and myself regarded by them as a completely worthless member of human society, no longer worthy of participation, is extremely painful to me; truly, it does not only rob me of the joys I expected of the future but it also poisons the past for me. The alliance the King is now concluding with the French is also not exactly calculated to keep me bound to life. The faces of those people were already

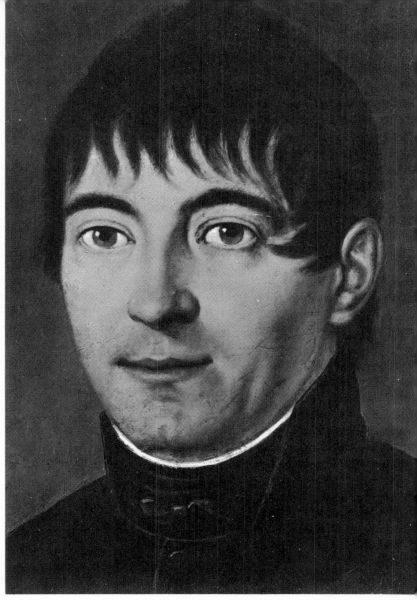

Alleged portrait of Kleist (Painting, 1811, probably by Michael Walbner; found in 1938)

repulsive to me when I met them, now if they met me in the
street I would be overcome by a physical sensation which I may
not name here. Of course it is true that, like them, I lacked the
strength to engage again; but I feel all too much that the will
which lives in my breast is other than the will of those who
make that clever comment: to the effect that I may have nothing
more to do with them. After all, if the King concludes this
alliance, what more can one do with him? The time is now upon
us when for one's loyalty to him, self-sacrifice, constancy and
all the other bourgeois virtues, one can come to the gallows,
condemned by him, himself. Add to this that I have found a
lady whose soul flies like a young eagle, such as I have never
found in my life before; who understands my sorrow as an
exalted, firmly rooted and incurable one, and therefore, although she would have enough means to make me happy here,
wishes to die with me; who grants me the unprecedented joy of
allowing herself to be plucked, for this purpose, as lightly from
a situation completely devoid of desire as a violet from a
meadow; who for my sake alone is leaving a father who adores
her, a man who was generous enough to resign her to me, a
child as beautiful and more beautiful than the morning sun: and
you will understand that my whole joyful care can only be to
find an abyss deep enough to fling myself into with her. Adieu
once more!"

On 20 November they drove to an inn on the Wannsee, ate
together "very happily" as the report went, drank coffee, then
wrote letters in their room and went to sleep. Next day they
paid their account to the innkeeper, asked for a messenger to
take their letters to Berlin, ate again and drank coffee and then
went together to the lake shore some fifty paces away. Two
shots were heard and the waitress running to the spot found
both on the ground. Kleist had shot Henriette Vogel through
the left breast into the heart and then himself in the head,
through the mouth. Both died instantaneously. Kleist was 34,
Henriette 31. They were both buried in a single grave on the site

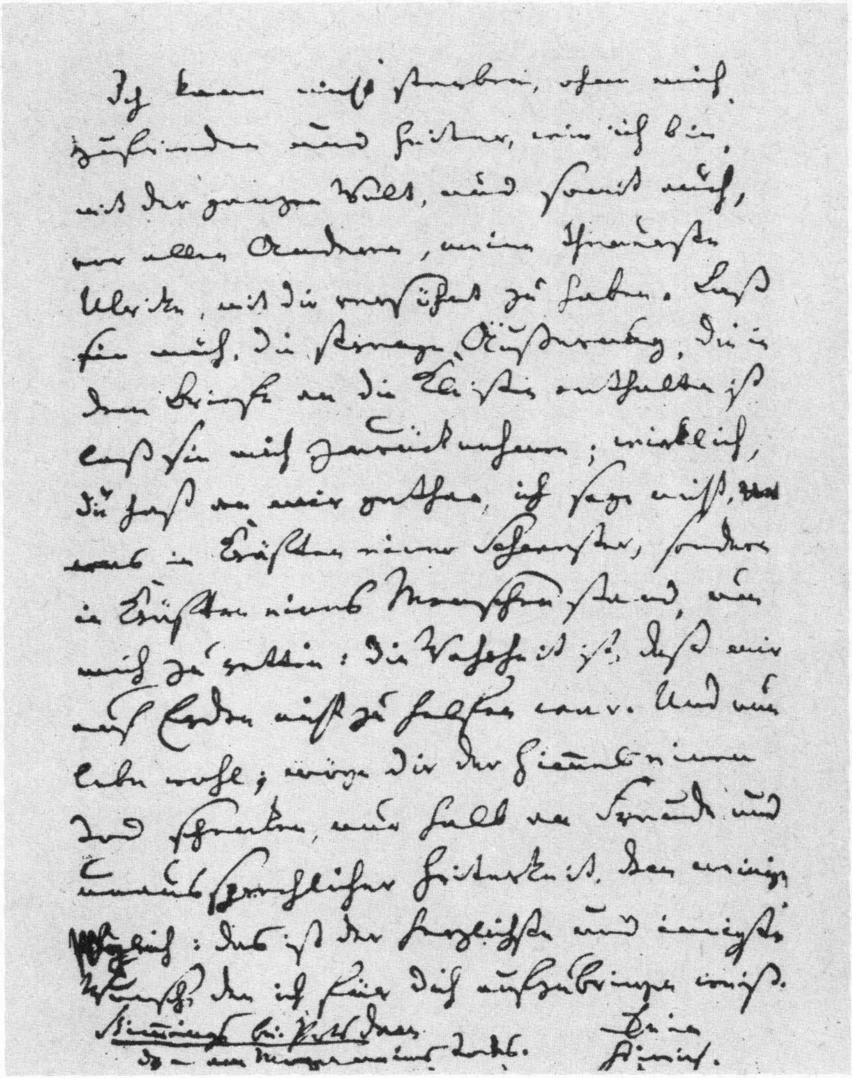

Ich kann nicht sterben, ohne mich,
zufrieden und heiter, wie ich bin,
mit der ganzen Welt, und somit auch,
vor allen Anderen, meine theuerste
Ulrike, mit Dir versöhnt zu haben. Laß
sie mich, die strenge Äußerung, die in
dem Briefe an die Kleisten enthalten ist,
laß sie mich zurücknehmen; wirklich,
Du hast an mir gethan, ich sage nicht,
in Kräften einer Schwester, sondern
in Kräften eines Menschen stand, um
mich zu retten: die Wahrheit ist, daß mir
auf Erden nicht zu helfen war. Und nun
lebe wohl; möge Dir der Himmel einen
Tod schenken, nur halb an Freude und
unaussprechlicher Heiterkeit, dem meinigen
gleich: das ist der herzlichste und innigste
Wunsch, den ich für Dich aufzubringen weiß.
Stimmings bei Potsdam d. — am Morgen meines Todes.
Dein
Heinrich.

Kleist's farewell letter to his step-sister Ulrike

of the murder and suicide. In the Vogels' Berlin flat Kleist had burned papers, letters and manuscripts, probably including his two-volume *Roman* (novel).

In Berlin, which was not a metropolis in the modern sense, the death of the two aroused a certain sensation. Among Kleist's friends and acquaintances, people were struck by the time of the catastrophe; it had always been feared that he would carry out his threat of death, but not now and in Henriette Vogel's company. It is difficult to form any clear judgement of Frau Vogel's character; some describe her as highly talented, noble, fanatical, others speak of a hysteric who had been involved with several men. For Kleist she was the chance, and for that reason welcome, partner in a deed which had something miserable and tragic about it and would darken the peculiar purity of his being, if it were not that the frenzied over-excitement of which he was capable has to be laid in the balance. Those who saw further, like Brentano, recognised that for Kleist the method of death was incidental; that he actually died of himself, of unfulfilled ambition, failed vocation and despair as to his capabilities. Fouqué the pious Christian promised to pray for Kleist. Arnim blamed Kleist's selfishness in that he committed himself to no trend and thought nothing of his friends' opinions. What sounds very understanding is Varnhagen's remark: "After everything that Pfuel and Brentano have told me of his qualities and his ultimate fate, I need no explanation; to me the paths whose goal is of this nature are not strange . . . but how greatly the poor man must have suffered on the extreme brink, when he was able to decide to destroy with him the talent he worshipped." Finally, Adam Müller thought that Kleist's heart was broken, his powers crippled before he took a decision which he "carried out not without conflict with his better nature."

Kleist had put his regular affairs in order, an acquaintance had been asked to pay the barber from money left ready, since he had forgotten to do so. Kleist's landlord received a token. But he wrote his last letter to Ulrike, really no more than a note, and here he said with the clarity of vision peculiar to him that there was no help left for him on earth:

"I cannot die, content and cheerful as I am, without being reconciled with the whole world and therefore also before all else, my dearest Ulrike, with you. Let me take back the stern remarks contained in the letter to Marie von Kleist, let me take them back; really, you have done for me — I shall not say all that lies in the power of a sister, but in the power of a human being, to save me: the truth is that there was no help for me on earth. And now farewell; may heaven grant you a death only half what mine is in happiness and inexpressible good cheer: that is the most heartfelt and fervent wish I could express for you.

Your
Heinrich

Stimmings near Potsdam
On the morning of my death."

148

Chronological Table

1777   Bernd Wilhelm Heinrich von Kleist born on 18 October, son of Captain Joachim Friedrich von Kleist and his second wife Juliane Ulrike, neé von Pannwitz, in Frankfurt-an-der-Oder. Of his two half and five full brothers and sisters, Ulrike (1774—1849) was his favourite sister.

1788   18 June. His father died.
        Kleist's education put in the hands of the Reverend S. H. Catel in Berlin.

1792   1 June. Entered Guards Regiment in Potsdam as Lance-Corporal.

1793–95 Took part in the Rhine Campaign.

1793   3 February. His mother died, Kleist on leave. First surviving letter, to his aunt, describing his return journey to Frankfurt-am-Main.

1797   7 March. Promotion to Lieutenant.
        Journey to the Harz with Rühle von Lilienstern. Mathematical and scientific studies.
        Friendship with Peter von Gualtieri and his sister Marie (Marie von Kleist) and Adolphine von Werdeck.

1799   March. Kleist left and spent three terms studying (Kameralia and Jus) at the national university in Frankfurt-an-der-Oder.
        Friendship and betrothal to Wilhelmine von Zenge.

1800   Mid—August. Returned to Berlin.
        End of August—October. Würzburg journey in company with his friend Brockes. Draft of *Familie Ghonorez*. Plan for an Amazon play *(Penthesilea)*. Study of Rousseau and Kant.
        1 November. Appointment as a trainee in the Prussian Ministry of Economics.

| 1801 | March. Kant crisis. (Letters of 22 and 23 March) Portrait miniature of Kleist sent to Wilhelmine. |

1801   March. Kant crisis. (Letters of 22 and 23 March)
Portrait miniature of Kleist sent to Wilhelmine.

April. With Ulrike via Dresden, Halberstadt (staying with Gleim), Göttingen, Mainz and Strasbourg, to Paris.

July—November in Paris. Work on *Robert Guiskard*. First version of *Verlobung in St. Domingo*.

November. Return to Frankfurt am Main. Travelled on, alone, to Switzerland (Bern, Thun). Associated with Heinrich Zschokke, Ludwig Wieland, Heinrich Gessner.

1802   From February. Kleist living on island in Aare, near Thun. Work on *Zerbrochener Krug* and *Guiskard*. Completion of *Familie Schroffenstein*. New plans *(Amphitryon, Leopold von Österreich, Peter der Einsiedler)*.

July—August: ill, in Bern.

October. To Weimar. Work on *Robert Guiskard*.

1803   January—early March. With Wieland in Ossmannstedt. Luise Wieland's love.

February. *Familie Schroffenstein* published (Bern and Zurich, anonymous).

Mid—March. Departure for Leipzig, Dresden. Association with Henriette von Schlieben. Suicide plans.

July—September. Walking tour with Pfuel to Bern, Milan, Geneva, Paris.

October. *Guiskard* manuscripts destroyed in Paris. Alone to Boulogne-sur-Mer. Physical and psychological collapse. Return to Germany.

1804   In Mainz. In the care of Dr. Wedekind.

Mid—June. Return to Berlin.

22 June. Interview with Adjutant von Köckeritz in Charlottenburg Castle.

Autumn. Reentered Prussian Government Service.

1805	Early May. To Königsberg as day-wage junior in Crown land chamber. Work on *Michael Kohlhaas, Amphitryon, Marquise von O.* and *Penthesilea.*
1806	August. Kleist on leave. Final renunciation of civil service career.
	October. Military collapse of Prussia.
1807	January. Attempted return to Berlin.
	February—July. Kleist imprisoned by the French. In Joux and Châlons-sur-Marne.
	Spring. *Amphitryon* published by Adam Müller in Dresden.
	August. Return to Germany. Kleist resident in Dresden, associated with C. G. Körner, Adam Müller, Sophie von Haza, Baron von Buol, Ludwig Tieck, Varnhagen.
	Completion of *Penthesilea* and *Käthchen von Heilbronn.*
1808	January—December. Kleist published monthly *Phöbus* with Adam Müller (including parts of his own works: *Penthesilea, Der zerbrochene Krug, Michael Kohlhaas, Robert Guiskard* fragment etc.)
	2 March. *Zerbrochener Krug* put on in Weimar by Goethe.
	Autumn Fair. *Penthesilea* published (Tübingen, by Cotta). *Hermannsschlacht* written.
1809	End of April. To Austria with Dahlmann.
	25 May. Visit to the battlefield of Aspern.
	June—October. In Prague. A journal, *Germania,* planned. Political poems, *Catechism for the Germans.* Kleist ill.
	End of year. Back in Frankfurt a. d. O.
1810	29 January. Return to Berlin. Associated with Adam Müller, Achim von Arnim, Clemens Brentano, Bernhard Anselm Weber, Fouqué, Rahel, Varnhagen.
	Autumn Fair. First volume of *Tales* published in Berlin, by Reimer. (Contents: *Michael Kohlhaas, Marqui-*

se von O., *Das Erdbeben in Chili*); *Käthchen von Heilbronn* published (also by Reimer).

1 October. The *Berliner Abendblätter* first published.

1811   30 March. Last number of *Berliner Abendblätter*. Dispute with Hardenberg over a pension.

Spring Fair. Publication of *Der zerbrochene Krug* and Vol. 2 of *Tales*, containing *Verlobung in St Domingo, Das Bettelweib von Locarno, Der Findling, Die heilige Cäcilie, Der Zweikampf.*

Summer and autumn. Associated with Marie von Kleist, Gneisenau, Henriette Vogel.

21 November. Suicide on Wannsee near Berlin.

1821   Publication of *Unpublished writings,* edited by Ludwig Tieck (including first impressions of the *Hermannsschlacht* and *Der Prinz von Homburg*).

Comments

Johann Wolfgang von Goethe

I have a right to reproach Kleist, because I have loved and praised him; but whether because his education, as is now the case with so many, was disturbed by the times, or for whatever other reason; enough, he has not fulfilled his promise. His hypochondria is too bad; it is destroying him as a man and as a writer.

Conversation with Falk, 1809

Clemens Brentano

Yesterday I received from Savigny the news that Heinrich von Kleist had shot himself a fortnight ago. This news horrified me at least as much as a pistol shot. The poor good fellow, his poetic cloth was too short for him and all his life he tried harder than any other modern poet to cut his coat according to its measure. It all came to this simply because he knew and loved no truly sincere people and was boundlessly vain.

To Achim von Arnim, 10 December 1811

Friedrich Hebbel

Reading Heinrich von Kleist's Tales has refreshed and truly encouraged me. That is what all genuine works of genius do for me; they are inexhaustible. Kleist is my model, insofar as one can have a model; there is more life packed into a single one of his episodes than in three parts of one of our modern novelist's books. He always describes the *inner* and the *outer* together, one by means of the other, and this is the only right way . . .

To Elise Lensing, 17 May 1837

Theodor Fontane

Even the firm enthusiasts who have been solicitous, over a number of years, to pay off the old Kleist national debt honourably, have as far as I know made no attempt to celebrate or justify the introductory scenes or the direct effect they produce. Although such an attempt is not really necessary. The play itself undertakes the task of restoring the balance. It expresses from one act to the next a growing, retroactive power which is so great, so captivating, that we not only throw off the last remnants of displeasure aroused in us by the romantic and apparently arbitrary exposition, but also finally come round to the half reluctant, half cheerful admission that if we want the play in its beauty and power at all, then we must also want what vexed us in it. A triumph of the art which is expressed in all Kleist's work, but perhaps most of all in this *Prince of Homburg*.

Theatre review 1976

Franz Kafka

Read the opening of *Michael Kohlhaas* in the Toynbee Hall. Total and utter failure. Poorly selected, poorly executed, finally pointlessly adrift in the text ... And in the afternoon I was already quivering with the desire to read, could scarcely keep my mouth shut.

Diaries, 11 December 1913

Rainer Maria Rilke

The Kleist was good, believe me ... the likes of us are nothing by comparison but pipsqueaks — now your taste has been ruined for his astringency by a certain poet whom you translate, but one day you must come upon the *Prince of Homburg*, the *Guiskard* fragment, and take a cool, new look ... It is all quite marvellous, and done so blindly and purely, wrenched from the depths of a hard nature ... when one remembers that Fouqué was his contemporary, and Frau von Fouqué too ... one is suddenly bowled over by what it means to be a man like that at the turn of the 19th century.

To Princess Marie von Thurn und Taxis-Hohenlohe, 27. 12. 1913

Thomas Mann

So I have loved and forgotten this play and praised it while it was forgotten, because there was no time or opportunity to see it, to read it again. Now a memorial celebration has made me take the time and the opportunity; I re-read it — and the natural law of my inner relationship to this thing has stood the test; I am ravished, I burn. It has the wittiest and most charming, the cleverest, most profound and loveliest dramatic action in the world. I knew I loved it — praise be! I now know why again.

Amphitryon. A Reconquest. 1926

Konrad Weiß

This writer does not send ideas to the divinity but only a single messenger, namely himself. Kleist is much more than an idea which is generally advocated, because he is as it were smaller, or because he is more definite. He is the great poetic spirit . . . His ideas, his inmost feelings are to some degree his female charatters. Just as they confide, give and receive glory, standing powerless and yet as the inmost power in simile and story, even as, with Penthesilea between nature and history, they recognize the most intimate bond of love only in conflict, or even as if struck blind, so in Kleist everything is his philosophy of the world — not philosophy as an idea, but as history and reality, or as the purest vote of confidence in existence.

Deutschlands Morgenspiegel. 1938

Bibliography

This bibliography is intended as a first guide and introduction. It offers the reader a starting point on the way to the many branches of Kleist research.

1. Bibliographies and Research Reports

Sembdner, Helmut: Kleist-Bibliographie 1803—1862. Heinrich von Kleists Schriften in frühen Drucken und Erstveröffentlichungen. Stuttgart 1966

Minde-Pouet, Georg: Kleist-Bibliographie 1914—1937. In: Jahrbuch (Annual Reports) der Kleist-Gesellschaft: 1921, p 89—169; 1922, p 112—163; 1923/24, p 181—230; 1929/30, p 60—193; 1933/37, 186—263

Rothe, Eva: Kleist Bibliographie 1945—60. In: Jahrbuch der Deutschen Schiller-Gesellschaft (Annual Report of the German Schiller Society) 5 (1961), p 414—547

Kluckhohn, Paul: Kleist-Forschung 1926—1943. In the Deutsche Vierteljahrsschrift 21 (1943), Reference Vol. p 45—87

Kreuzer, H: Kleist-Literatur 1955—1960. In Deutschunterricht 13 (1961), p 116—135

Lefèvre, Manfred: Kleist-Forschung 1961—1967. In Colloquia Germanica 3 (1969), p 1—86

Sembdner, Helmut: Neuentdeckte Schriften Heinrich von Kleists. In: Euphorion 53 (1959) p 175—194

Rothe, Eva and *Helmut Sembdner:* Die Kleist-Handschriften und ihr Verbleib. In: Jahrbuch der Deutschen Schiller-Gesellschaft 8 (1964), p 324—343

Kreuzer, Hans Joachim: Kleists Dramenhandschriften. Probleme ihrer Datierung. In: Kolloquium über Probleme der Kommentierung. Bonn 1971. p 75—94

Schanze, Helmut: Index zu Heinrich von Kleist: Sämtliche Erzählungen, Erzählvarianten, Anekdoten. Frankfurt a. M., Bonn 1969

Kanzog, Klaus: Prolegomena zu einer historisch-kritischen Ausgabe der Werke Heinrich von Kleists. Theorie und Praxis einer modernen Klassiker-Edition. Munich 1970

2. Editions of the Works

Werke. In coll. with *Georg Minde-Pouet* and *Reinhold Steig* ed. by *Erich Schmidt.* Kritisch durchgesehene und erläuterte Gesamtausgabe. 5 Vols. Leipzig 1904/05. 2nd Ed. 7 Vols, Leipzig 1936—38

Sämtliche Werke. Ed by *Wilhelm Herzog* 6 Vols, Leipzig 1908—1911

Sämtliche Werke. Ed by *Friedrich Michael.* Leipzig 1927

Sämtliche Werke in einem Band. Ed by *Erwin Laaths.* Munich 1954

Sämtliche Werke und Briefe. Ed. by *Helmut Sembdner.* 2 Vols. Munich

1954. New ed. entitled: Sämtliche Werke und Briefe. 2., vermehrte und auf Grund der Erstdrucke und Handschriften völlig revidierte Aufl. Munich 1961. 5th Ed. 1970. — Paperback ed. entitled: Werke und Briefe. 7 vols Munich 1964

Cf. *Sembdner, Helmut:* Kleists Interpunktion. Zur Neuausgabe seiner Werke. In: Jahrbuch der Deutschen Schiller-Gesellschaft 6 (1962) p 229—259. Repr. in: Heinrich von Kleist. Aufsätze und Essays. Ed. by *Walter Müller-Seidel.* Darmstadt 1967. p 605—634

Gesammelte Werke in vier Bänden. Ed. and introduced by *Heinrich Deiters.* Berlin 1955

Sämtliche Werke in einem Band. Nach dem Text der Ausgaben letzter Hand und Berücksichtigung der Erstdrucke und Handschriften. With epilogue and commentary by *Curt Grützmacher,* Munich 1967

Sämtliche Werke. Dramen. Erzählungen. Gedichte. Briefe. Mit einer Einf. in Leben und Werk, ed. by *K. F. Reinking.* Wiesbaden 1972

3. Facsimile Editions

Berliner Abendblätter. With an epilogue, ed. by *Georg Minde-Pouet.* Leipzig 1925 (Faksimiledrucke literarischer Seltenheiten. 2)

Berliner Abendblätter. Herausgegeben von Heinrich von Kleist. Epilogue and Sources by *Helmut Sembdner* (Photo-mechanical reproduction). Darmstadt 1959

Germania an ihre Kinder. Facsimile of the first edition of 1813. With a foreword, ed. by *Georg Minde-Pouet.* Leipzig 1927

Das Käthchen von Heilbronn. (Abdruck der Phöbusfassung. Reprograph. of Halle ed. 1813) Appendage to *Friedrich Röbbeling,* Kleists Käthchen von Heilbronn. Walluf b. Wiesbaden 1973

Der zerbrochene Krug. Eine Nachbildung der Handschrift. Ed by *Paul Hoffmann,* Weimar 1941

Penthesilea. Ein Trauerspiel. (Facsimile of Tübingen ed. 1808) [with supplement] Dokumente und Zeugnisse. Ed by *Helmut Sembdner.* Frankfurt a. M. 1967

Phöbus, ein Journal für die Kunst, herausgegeben von Heinrich von Kleist und Adam H. Müller. Facsimile reprint ed. by *Fritz Strich,* Munich 1924

4. Biographical evidence

Letters. Ed. and introd. by *Friedrich Michael.* Leipzig 1925

Geschichte meiner Seele. Ideen magazin. Das Lebenszeugnis der Briefe. Ed. by *Helmut Sembdner.* Bremen 1959

Biedermann, Flodard Frh. von: Kleists Gespräche. Leipzig 1912

Sembdner, Helmut: Kleists Lebensspuren. Dokumente und Berichte der Zeitgenossen. Bremen 1957 (Sammlung Dieterich. 172) 2nd rev. and expanded ed. 1964. — As paperback and Vol. 8 of the dtv edition of the works, under the title: Heinrich von Kleists Lebensspuren. Revised and expanded ed. Munich 1969

Erlösser, Arthur: Neue Kleist-Miniaturen. In: Jahrbuch der Kleist-Gesellschaft 1923/24 p 142—145 with ill.

Meyer, Hellmut: Ein neues Bild von Heinrich von Kleist. In the Annual Report of the Kleist-Gesellschaft 1938, p 62—70

Rothe, Eva: Die Bildnisse Heinrich von Kleists. Mit neuen Dokumenten zu Kleists Kriegsgefangenschaft. In: Jahrbuch der Deutschen Schiller-Gesellschaft 5 (1961) p 136—187

5. Complete accounts

Brahm, Otto: Heinrich von Kleist. Berlin 1884

Rahmer, Sigismund: Heinrich von Kleist als Menschen und Dichter. Nach neuen Quellenforschungen. Berlin 1909

Meyer-Benfey, Heinrich: Kleists Leben und Werke. Göttingen 1911

Herzog, Wilhelm: Heinrich von Kleist. Sein Leben und sein Werk. Munich 1911

Gundolf, Friedrich: Heinrich von Kleist. Berlin 1922

Witkop, Philipp: Heinrich von Kleist. Leipzig 1922

Muschg, Walter: Kleist. Zürich 1923

Braig, Friedrich: Heinrich von Kleist. Munich 1925

Bertram, Ernst: Heinrich von Kleist. Eine Rede. Bonn 1925

Ayrault, Roger: Heinrich von Kleist. Paris 1934

Heiseler, Bernt von: Heinrich von Kleist. Stuttgart 1939 (Die Dichter der Deutschen. 3)

Kommerell, Max: Die Sprache und das Unaussprechliche. Eine Betrachtung über Heinrich von Kleist. In: *Kommerell,* Geist und Buchstabe der Dichtung. Frankfurt a. M. 1940 p 243—317 — 4th impr. 1956

Uyttersprot, H.: Heinrich von Kleist. De mens en het werk. Bruges 1948

Wolff, Hans M.: Heinrich von Kleist. Die Geschichte eines Schaffens. Bern 1954

Maaß, Joachim: Kleist, die Fackel Preußens. Eine Lebensgeschichte. Vienna—Munich—Basel 1957

Michaelis, Rolf: Heinrich von Kleist. Velber 1965 (Friedrichs Dramatiker des Welttheaters. 5)

Gerlach, Kurt: Heinrich von Kleist. Sein Leben und Schaffen in neuer Sicht. Dortmund 1971

6. Assessments and interpretations

Hoffmann, Paul: Kleist in Paris. Berlin 1924

Minde-Pouet, Georg: Kleists letzte Stunden. Part 1: Das Akten-Material. Berlin 1925 (Schriften der Kleist-Gesellschaft 5)

Fricke, Gerhard: Gefühl und Schicksal bei Heinrich von Kleist. Studien über den inneren Vorgang im Leben und Schaffen des Dichters. Berlin 1929 (Neue Forschungen. 3) — Unaltered photomechanical reprod. Darmstadt 1963

Lugowski, Clemens: Wirklichkeit und Dichtung. Untersuchungen zur Wirklichkeitsauffassung Heinrich von Kleists. Leipzig 1936

Martini, Fritz: Heinrich von Kleist und die geschichtliche Welt. Berlin 1940 (Germanische Studien. 225)

Wolff, H. M.: Heinrich von Kleist. Die Geschichte seines Schaffens. Bern 1954

Koch, Friedrich: Heinrich von Kleist. Bewußtsein und Wirklichkeit. Stuttgart 1958

Ide, H.: Der junge Kleist ". . . in dieser wandelbaren Zeit . . ." Würzburg 1961

Müller-Seidel, Walter: Verstehen und Erkennen. Eine Studie über Heinrich von Kleist. Cologne—Graz 1961

Müller, J. K.-H.: Die Rechts- und Staatsauffassung Heinrich von Kleists. Bonn 1962.

Haupt, Gunther: Heinrich von Kleist in Berlin. Berlin 1963, Kleist und die Gesellschaft. Eine Diskussion. Berlin, 1965 (with contributions by E. Catholy, K. O. Conrady, H. Ide and W. Müller-Seidel)

Heinrich von Kleist. Aufsätze und Essays. Ed. by *Walter Müller-Seidel.* Darmstadt 1967

Hoffmeister, E.: Täuschung und Wirklichkeit bei Heinrich von Kleist. Bonn 1968

Belgardt, Raimund: Kleists Weg zur Wahrheit. Irrtum und Wahrheit als Denkformen und Strukturmöglichkeit. In: Zs. f. dt. Philologie 92 (1973), p 161—184

Reske, Hermann: Heinrich von Kleist in Thun. Die Geburt des Genius. Bern, Stuttgart 1972

Sembdner, Helmut: In Sachen Kleist. Beiträge zur Forschung. Munich 1974

Kunert, Günter: Pamphlet für Kleist. In: Sinn und Form 27 (1975), p. 1091—1097

7. Relationships and Influences

Brand, Hans Erich: Kleist und Dostojewskij. Extreme Formen der Wirklichkeit als Ausdrucksmittel religiöser Anschauungen. Bonn 1970

Sembdner, Helmut: Fouqués unbekanntes Wirken für Heinrich von Kleist. In: Jahrbuch der Deutschen Schiller-Gesellschaft 2 (1958), p 83—113

Mommsen, Katharina: Kleists Kampf mit Goethe. Heidelberg 1974 (Poesie und Wissenschaft. 27)

Sembdner, Helmut: Heinrich von Kleist im Urteil der Brüder Grimm. Unbekannte Rezessionen. In: Jahrbuch der Deutschen Schiller-Gesellschaft 9 (1965), p 420—446

Kreuzer, H.: Hebbel und Kleist. In: Deutschunterricht 13 (1961) p 92—115

Cassirer, Ernst: Heinrich von Kleist und die Kantische Philosophie. Berlin 1919 (Philosophische Vorträge, 22)

Muth, Ludwig: Kleist und Kant. Versuch einer neuen Interpretation. Cologne 1954

Reiss, Gunter: Sündenfall-Modell und Romanform. Zur Integration von Kleists Marionettentheater-Thematik im Werk Thomas Manns. In: Jahrbuch der Deutschen Schiller-Gesellschaft 13 (1969), p 426—453

160

Mühlher, Robert: Kleists und Adam Müllers Freundschaftskrise. Zwei unge-
druckte Briefe Müllers zur Geschichte des "Phöbus". In Euphorion 45 (1950),
p 450—470

Lüders, E. M.: Kleist, Rilke und der Tänzer. Zu einer Ästhetischen Frage der
Modernen Dichtung. In: Deutsche Vierteljahrsschrift 42 (1968), p 515—552

Xylander, Oskar Ritter von: Heinrich von Kleist und J. J. Rousseau. Berlin
1937 (Germanische Studien 193) — Repr. Nendeln/Liechtenstein 1967

Leber, E.: Das Bild des Menschen in Schillers und Kleists Dramen. Bern
1969

Sembdner, Helmut: Schütz-Lacrimas. Das Leben des Romantikerfreundes,
Poeten und Literaturkritikers Wilhelm von Schütz. Mit unbekannten Briefen
und Kleist-Rezensionen. Berlin 1974

Corssen, Meta: Kleist und Shakespeare. Weimar 1930 (Forschungen zur
neueren Literaturgeschichte. 61)

Schoch, M.: Kleist und Sophokles. Zürich 1952

8. Studies

a) On Kleist's complete oeuvre

Hohoff, Curt: Komik und Humor bei Heinrich von Kleist. Berlin 1937
(Germanische Studien. 184)

Dürst, Rolf: Heinrich von Kleist, Dichter zwischen Ursprung und Endzeit.
Kleists Werk im Licht idealistischer Eschatalogie. Bern—Munich 1965

Kreutzer, Hans Joachim: Die dichterische Entwicklung Heinrich von
Kleists. Untersuchungen zu seinen Briefen und zu Chronologie und Aufbau
seiner Werke. Berlin—Bielefeld—Munich 1967 (Philologische Studien und
Quellen. 41)

Lupi, Sergio: Conscienza e inconscio nell'arte di Heinrich von Kleist.
Florence 1969 (Saggi di letterature straniere. 1)

Reske, H.: Traum und Wirklichkeit im Werk Heinrich von Kleists. Stuttgart—Berlin—Cologne—Münster 1969

Skrotzki, Ditmar: Die Gebärde des Errötens im Werk Heinrich von Kleists.
Marburg 1971

Bartels, Siegfried: Vermittlung der Gegensätze in der Dichtung Heinrich von
Kleists. Bürgerliche Subjektivität im Konflikt mit höfischen Machtverhältnis-
sen. Waldacher 1973

Schmidt, Jochen: Heinrich von Kleist. Studien zu seiner poetischen Verfah-
rensweise. Tübingen 1974

Dettmering, Peter: Heinrich von Kleist. Zur Psychodynamik in seiner
Dichtung. Munich 1975 (sammlung dialog. 74)

Reusner, Ernst von: Satz, Gestalt, Schicksal. Untersuchungen über die
Struktur in der Dichtung Kleists. Berlin 1961 (Quellen und Forschungen zur
Sprach- und Kulturgesch. d. germ. Völker. NF 6)

Holz, Hans Heinz: Macht und Ohnmacht der Sprache. Untersuchungen
zum Sprachverhältnis und Stil Heinrich von Kleists. Frankfurt a. M. — Bonn
1962

Spältli, Jakob: Interpretationen zu Heinrich von Kleists Verhältnis zur Sprache. Bern 1975

Koopmann, H.: Das "Rätselhafte Faktum" und seine Vorgeschichte. Zum analytischen Charakter der Novellen Heinrich von Kleists. In: Zs. f. dt. Philologie 84 (1965) p 508—550
Moering, Michael: Witz und Ironie in der Prosa Heinrich von Kleists. Munich 1972
Müller-Salget, Klaus: Das Prinzip der Doppeldeutigkeit in Kleists Erzählungen. In Zs. f. dt. Philologie 92 (1973) p 185—211
Reinert, Claus: Detektivliteratur bei Sophokles, Schiller und Kleist oder Das Rätsel der Wahrheit und das Abenteuer des Erkennens. Kronberg 1975 (Theorie — Kritik — Geschichte 8)

Lukács, Georg: Die Tragödie Heinrich von Kleists. In: Lukács, Deutsche Literatur in zwei Jahrhunderten. Neuwied—Berlin 1964. p 201—231 (Werke 7)
Kohrs, Ingrid: Das Wesen des Tragischen im Drama Heinrich von Kleists. Dargestellt an Interpretationen von *Penthesilea* und *Prinz von Homburg.* Marburg 1951
Wiese, Benno von: Der Tragiker Heinrich von Kleist und sein Jahrhundert. In: *Wiese,* Die deutsche Tragödie von Lessing bis Hebbel. Hamburg 1961. p 275—344
Streller, S.: Das dramatische Werk Heinrich von Kleists. Berlin 1966
Donner, Wolf: Der naive Typus als dramatische Figur bei Schiller, Kleist, Grillparzer und Wagner. Cologne 1967
Dethlefsen, Dirk: Zu Metrum und Rhythmus des Blankverses in den Dramen Heinrich von Kleists. Munich 1970
Scheufele, Theodor: Die theatralische Physiognomie der Dramen Kleists. Untersuchungen zum Problem des Theatralischen im Drama. Meisenheim 1975 (Deutsche Studien. 24)
Labhardt, Robert: Metapher und Geschichte. Kleists dramatische Metaphorik bis zur *Penthesilea* als Wiederspiegelung seiner geschichtlichen Position. Kronberg 1976

b) On individual works

Sembdner, Helmut: Kleist und Falk. Zur Entstehungsgeschichte von Kleists *Amphitryon.* In: Jahrbuch der Deutschen Schiller-Gesellschaft 13 (1969), p 361—396
Müller-Seidel, Walter: Die Vermischung des Komischen mit dem Tragischen in Kleists Lustspiel *Amphitryon.* In: Jahrbuch der Deutschen Schiller-Gesellschaft 5 (1961), p 118—135
Aggeler, Jürg: Der Weg von Kleists *Alkmene.* Bern—Frankfurt a. M. 1962
Grathoff, Dirk: Die Zensurkonflikte der *Berliner Abendblätter.* In: Beziehung von Journalismus und Öffentlichkeit bei Heinrich von Kleist. In: Idiologiekritische Studien zur Literatur 1972, p 35—168
Wiese, Benno von: Heinrich von Kleist: *Das Erdbeben in Chile.* In: *Wiese,* Die deutsche Novelle von Goethe bis Kafka. Vol. 2 Hamburg, 1962. p 53—70

Kunz, Josef: Die Gestaltung des tragischen Geschehens in Kleists *Erdbeben in Chile.* In: Gratulatio 1963. p 145—170

Lucas, R. S.: Studies in Kleist. *Das Erdbeben in Chile.* In Deutsche Vierteljahrsschrift 44 (1970), p 145—170

Seeba, Hinrich C.: Der Sündenfall des Verdachts. Identitätskrise und Sprachskepsis in Kleists *Familie Schroffenstein.* In: Deutsche Vierteljahrsschrift 44 (1970), p 64—100

Moore, Erna: Heinrich von Kleists *Findling.* Psychologie des Verhängnisses. In: Colloquia Germanica 1974, p 275—297

Röbbeling, Friedrich: Kleists *Käthchen von Heilbronn.* Mit einem Anhang (Abdruck der Phöbusfassung. Reprograph. of Halle Ed. 1913) Walluf b. Wiesbaden 1973

Die Quellen zu Heinrich von Kleists *Michael Kohlhaas;* Ed. by *Rudolf Schlösser.* Berlin 1913 (Kleine Texte für Vorlesungen und Übungen. 116)

Lucas, R. S.: Studies in Kleist: *Michael Kohlhaas.* In: Deutsche Vierteljahrsschrift 44 (1970), p 120—145

Müller, Richard Matthias: Kleists *Michael Kohlhaas.* In: Deutsche Vierteljahrsschrift 44 (1970), p 101—119

Horn, Peter: Was geht uns eigentlich der Gerechtigkeitsbegriff in Kleists Erzählung *Michael Kohlhaas* noch an? In: Acta Germanica 8 (1973), p 59—92

Kurth, Jörg: Über literaturwissenschaftliche Erkenntnis oder Was geht mich *Michael Kohlhaas* an? Zürich 1975

Turk, Horst: Dramensprache als gesprochene Sprache. Untersuchungen zu Kleists *Penthesilea.* Bonn 1965 (Abhandlungen zur Kunst-, Musik- und Literaturwissenschaft. 31)

Durzak, Manfred: Das Gesetz der Athene und das Gesetz des Tanias. Zur Funktion des Mythischen in Kleists *Penthesilea.* In: Jahrbuch des Freien deutschen Hochstifts 1973, p 354—370

Wittkowski, Wolfgang: Absolutsgefühl und absolute Kunst in Kleists *Prinz Friedrich von Homburg.* In: Deutschunterricht 1 (1961), p 27—71

Hohendahl, P. U.: Der Pass des Grafen Horn. Ein Aspekt des Politischen in *Prinz Friedrich von Homburg.* In: German Quarterly 41 (1968), p 167—176

Schweizer, K.: Heinrich von Kleist. *Prinz von Homburg.* Interpretation. Munich 1968

Thalheim, H.-G.: Kleists *Prinz Friedrich von Homburg.* In: *Thalheim,* Zur Literatur der Goethezeit. Berlin 1969, p 322—410

Ellis, J. M.: Kleist's *Prinz von Homburg.* A critical study. Berkeley — London 1970 (University of California Publications in Modern Philology. 97)

Hackert, Fritz: Kleists *Prinz von Homburg* in der Nachkriegs-Interpretation 1947—1972. Ein Literaturbericht. In: Zeitschrift für Literaturwissenschaft und Linguistik 3 (1973), p 53—80

Kleists Aufsatz *Über das Marionettentheater.* Studien und Interpretationen. Ed. with on epiloque by *Helmut Sembdner.* Berlin 1967

Kathan, Anton: Der Vorgang des Erkennens und das Formen des Bewußtseins in Kleists Gespräch *Über das Marionettentheater.* In: Vergleichen und verändern 1970, p 114—139

Schrimpf, H. J.: Kleist, *Der zerbrochene Krug.* In: Das deutsche Drama. Ed. *Benno von Wiese.* Vol. 1 Hamburg, 1958, p 339—362

Martini, Fritz: Kleists *Der zerbrochene Krug.* Bauformen des Lustspiels. In: Jahrbuch der Deutschen Schiller-Gesellschaft 9 (1969), p 373—419

Schneider, Karl Ludwig: Heinrich von Kleists Lustspiel *Der zerbrochene Krug.* In: Das deutsche Lustspiel. Ed. by *Hans Steffen,* Part 1 Göttingen, 1968, p 166—180

Delbrück, Hansgerd: Zur dramentypologischen Funktion von Sündenfall und Rechtfertigung in Kleists *Zerbrochener Kurg.* In: Deutsche Vierteljahrsschrift 45 (1971), p 706—756

Sembdner, Helmut: Heinrich von Kleist. *Der zerbrochene Krug.* Erläuterungen und Dokumente. Stuttgart 1973 (Universal-Bibliothek. 8123/23 a)

Delbrück, Hansgerd: Kleists Weg zur Komödie. Untersuchungen zur Stellung des *Zerbrochenen Kruges* in einer Typologie des Lustspiels. Tübingen 1974 (Studien zur deutschen Literatur. 38)

Roesch, Ewald: Bett und Richterstuhl. Gattungsgeschichtliche Überlegungen zu Kleists Lustspiel *Der zerbrochene Krug.* In: Kritische Bewahrung. Festschrift für Werner Schröder zum 60. Geburtstag. Berlin 1974, p 434—475

Wittkowski, Wolfgang: Die Heilige Cäcilie und *Der Zweikampf.* Kleists Legenden und die romantische Ironie. In: Colloquia Germanica 1972, p 17—58

9. Kleist's influence

Heinrich von Kleists Nachruhm. Eine Wirkungsgeschichte in Dokumenten. Ed by *Helmut Sembdner,* Bremen 1967

Kleist in Frankreich. Mit Beiträgen von *C. David, W. Wittkowski, L. J. Ryan.* Berlin 1969

Busch, Rolf: Imperialistische und faschistische Kleist-Rezeption 1890—1945. Eine ideologiekritische Untersuchung Frankfurt a. M. 1974 (Studien zur Germanistik)

Translations

a) Works

Three Stories. Ed. by *H. B. Garland.* Manchester 1953

The Prince of Homburg. A play in 5 acts. Translated, with an introduction by *Charles E. Passage.* New York 1956

Penthesilea. English version by *Humphrey Trevelyan.* In: *Bentley, Eric R.:* The Classic Theatre. 1959. vol. 2; p 313—507

The Broken Pitcher. A comedy of one act. Translated into English. Verse by *Bayard Quincy Morgan.* Chapel Hill 1961

The Broken Jug. English version by *Lawrence P. R. Wilson.* In: *Allen, John P.:* Four continental plays. 1964. p 1—66

Amphitryon. Ed. by *Keith A. Dickson.* London 1968

Michael Kohlhaas. Ed. by *J. Gearey.* New York 1968

The Marquise of O and Other Stories. Translated and with an introduction by *Martin Greenberg.* London 1973

b) Secondary literature

Blankenagel, John Carl: The Attitude of Heinrich von Kleist toward the problems of life. Göttingen 1917

Silz, Walter: Heinrich von Kleist's conception of the tragic. Göttingen—Baltimore 1923 (Hesperia. 12)

March, Richard: Heinrich von Kleist. Cambridge 1954

Helbing, Robert Eugene: Heinrich von Kleist's Way from Rationalism to Ethical Voluntarism. Stanford 1959

Gearey, John Edward: Philosophy and Form: an Analysis of the Basic Patterns in the Thought and Works of Heinrich von Kleist. Columbia 1959/60

Silz, Walter: Heinrich von Kleist. Studies in his Works and Literary Character. Philadelphia 1961

Stahl, Ernst L.: Heinrich von Kleist's Dramas. Oxford 1961

Richardson, Frank C.: Kleist in France. Chapel Hill 1962

Peters, F. G.: Kafka and Kleist. A literary relationship. In: Oxford Germ. Stud. 1 (1966), p 144—162

Garland, Mary: Kleist's Prinz Friedrich von Homburg. An Interpretation Through Word Pattern. The Hague—Paris 1968

Gearey, John: Heinrich von Kleist. A Study in Tragedy and Anxiety. Philadelphia 1968

Ellis, John Martin: Kleist's Prinz Friedrich von Homburg. A Critical Study. Berkeley 1970

Frank, Luanne Thornton: The Archetypal World of Heinrich von Kleist. University of Michigan 1970

Clouser, Rubin A: Counterpoint in the Works of Heinrich von Kleist. University of Kansas 1971

Turner, Jerry Marshall: Statements of Feeling and Reason in the dramas of Heinrich von Kleist. Vanderbilt University 1971

Flikkema, Eltjen John: The Function of the Death Motif in the Works of Heinrich von Kleist. Michigan State University 1972

Helbing, Robert E: The Major Works of Heinrich von Kleist. New York 1975

The Author

Curt Hohoff, born in Emden on 18 March 1913. Classical secondary school. Studied Germanistics in Münster, Berlin, Munich, Cambridge. Took his D. Phil. (Thesis: "Comedy and Humour in Heinrich von Kleist") and government examination in 1936. Free-lance author in Munich. 1939–1945, soldier. Has worked since for newspapers and broadcasting and written stories, essays and novels. Member of the Akademie der Künste in Berlin and of the Bayerische Akademie der Schönen Künste.

Sources of Illustrations

Ullstein-Bilderdienst: 9, 10, 15 (top), 21, 27, 29, 33, 38, 48, 49, 63, 65, 71, 75, 79, 87, 88, 93, 97, 105 (top), 111, 115, 119, 127, 141, 145
Historisches Bildarchiv: 31, 41, 57, 82, 95, 121
Historia-Photo: 13, 45, 52, 105 (bottom), 109, 118
Dr. Walter Boje: 77, 135
Kunsthalle Bremen: 91
Dr. J. Wilke: 15 (bottom)
Hellmut Meyer: 143